Evald Flisar

WORDS ABOVE THE CLOUDS

*Translated from the Slovene
by Timothy Pogacar*

tP
Texture Press
2017

Also by Evald Flisar

Tales of Wandering

My Father's Dreams

Three Loves, One Death

On the Gold Coast

A Journey Too Far

Enchanted Odysseus

The Sorcerer's Apprentice

Tea with the Queen

If I Only Had Time

The Girl Who Would Rather be Elsewhere

That's Where You'll Find Me

Alice in Crazyland

Collected Plays, Vol. 1

Collected Plays, Vol. 2

WORDS ABOVE THE CLOUDS
Copyright © Evald Flisar

Translation copyright © Timothy Pogacar
Timothy Pogacar has received a grant from the Slovenian Book Agency.

Originally published in Slovenia (European Union) as *Besede nad oblaki* (Ljubljana: Cankarjeva založba, 2015).

Published in the United States by
Texture Press, 1108 Westbrooke Terrace,
Norman, OK 73072

Editor
Susan Smith Nash, PhD
texturepress@beyondutopia.com

Cover design
Arlene Ang

Published with the financial assistance of Trubar Foundation, Ljubljana, Slovenia.

The names, characters, and events portrayed in these pages are the product of the author's imagination. Any resemblance to actual persons, living or dead, or to real events is entirely coincidental.

All rights reserved. Duplication or reproduction by any mechanical or electronic means is strictly prohibited, except for brief quotation by a reviewer, critic, or friend, or by use of Texture Press to publicize the work.

ISBN 978-1-945784-05-7

Contents

1. On the Way to Mom's
2. The Final Journey
3. Therapy
4. Journey into Silence
5. Devil's Work
6. Shades of Sorrow
7. Sex on Bali
8. The Best Actor
9. Key Vendors
10. Competition of Quotomaniacs
11. Inheritance
12. A Hollywood "Star's" Final Days
13. In *vino veritas*
14. A Bomb on Board
15. Side Effects
16. Pride Parade
17. Turbulence

"Ladies and gentlemen, this is your captain speaking. Welcome aboard Singapore Airlines flight 2191 from London to Singapore. We are currently flying at an altitude of 33,000 feet, at a speed of 620 miles an hour. We just passed over Belgium and are continuing across Germany towards the Carpathian Mountains and the Black Sea. The weather is good, although there is a carpet of clouds below us. As usual at this time of year, it is raining in Singapore. We don't expect significant changes, except over India, where we could encounter turbulence, though that shouldn't cause untoward problems. Significant tail winds will increase our speed, and we'll arrive in Singapore approximately twenty minutes ahead of schedule. That will make for a less stressful transfer for those passengers who are traveling on to Australia and to destinations in Southeast Asia. In a few minutes, the flight crew will be serving drinks and a light snack. Thank you for choosing Singapore Airlines. I wish you a pleasant flight. I will make further announcements as needed. In the meantime, please follow the cabin crew's directions."

"Ladies and gentlemen, this is the head steward speaking, in charge of the cabin crew that will be seeing to your comfort. I would once again like to remind you that smoking is prohibited on this flight, and that there are smoke alarms in all the restrooms. The fasten seatbelts sign is now off. You are free to move about the cabin, but we advise you to keep your seatbelt fastened during the flight, since we can encounter unexpected turbulence. You may now use your electronic devices. On the screen in front of you, you have a wide selection of films and video games for the children. If you need anything or for any reason you don't feel well, push the button above your seat and one of the flight attendants will come to you as soon as possible. Thank you for your attention. Relax and enjoy the flight."

1.

On the Way to Mom's

"Daddy?"

"Yes, Hugo?"

"Are you going to keep on reading?"

"No. I have had enough bad news." He folds the newspaper and stuffs it into the mesh pocket in front of him. "Go on."

"How do they make planes?"

"In a factory. Like most things."

"In one piece or a lot?"

"The number would amaze you."

"Tell me."

"You won't believe it."

"Why not?"

"Because you haven't gotten to such big numbers in school."

"But I'm tops in my class."

"That's true. The Boeing 747-400, the jumbo jet that we're flying to Australia is made of six million different parts."

"Is that a lot or a little?"

"It's so many that most people wouldn't believe it."

"But I believe you, daddy."

"That's nice."

"Because you always know everything."

"That's far from the truth, but it's nice that you believe me. One more thing. Half of the six million parts are rivets and screws."

"What are rivets?"

"Rivets are…let me think… a rivet is a kind of metal fastener with a wide head on one end that you shoot through a hole in two metal surfaces, and on the other side you flatten the end of the small metal tube into a second head, and then the metal surfaces are joined and can never come apart."

"Never?"

"Never. Except if someone makes a mistake."

"That means that the plane we're sitting in has a million and a half screws besides the rivets?"

"It's hard to believe, isn't it? Because it looks so compact."

"What's compact, daddy?"

"Something that looks like one piece."

"But it's really not?"

"In fact it's put together. Do you know that there're 172 miles of wires in this plane?"

"Why?"

"Because they're needed. And eight kilometers of pipes! Hard to imagine. The aluminum to construct the body altogether weighs sixty-six tons."

"Is that a lot or a little?"

"Enough to make you dizzy. But that's not all. The plane is twenty yards high. Just one wing weighs forty-three tons. The landing gear has sixteen tires. And there're two more in front on the nose gear strut."

"Daddy?"

"What?"

"How did we end up on the only plane like that in the world?"

"Hugo, right now there're 680 planes like this in the air. There's an average of 520 passengers on each one. That means that right now there are something more than 350,000 people in the air just in jumbo jets."

"Where are they flying?"

"Some here, others there."

"But not all to Australia?"

"To all ends of the earth. And not only that. There are 680 jumbo jets in the air every day. And altogether until now they've flown forty million miles."

"Is that a lot?"

"That's about the same as 80,000 flights to the moon and back. In that time, they've carried almost three and a half billion people, which is half of mankind."

"Half of mankind is always in the air?"

"No, Hugo. That's how many the jumbo jets have carried since they started flying. But jumbo jets are not the only planes in the air right now."

"No?"

"Every second there're between 6,000 and 11,000 planes in the air."

"So this second there are a whole lot of people above the clouds."

"I'd say so."

"Half of mankind?"

"Not that many. Something over a half million."

"And they're all flying somewhere?"

"Of course. Why else would they be in the air?"

"Every one with some place to go?"

"Exactly."

"Like the two of us?"

"Like the two of us."

"Daddy, why is this plane called a jumbo?"

"That's the name of the first elephant brought from Africa to Europe. He became very famous, and ever since then people have called very big things jumbo."

"Will you tell me about that?"

"Oh, that's a long story. Very interesting and long. Maybe later."

"Can I call you Jumbo, too?"

"No, I'm not that big."

"But you are."

10

"That's how I look to you, because you're small. If you look around the plane, you'll see quite a few dads bigger than me."

"But you're still the biggest."

"Come on."

"Daddy, I'm hungry."

"The food will be here soon. If you get up and look, you'll see they're serving it just ahead. If you're thirsty, I'll order juice."

"Where do they get all that food?"

"They load it before the plane takes off. Like the luggage. You know how much food they serve to the passengers on a flight like this?"

"A lot?"

"Six tons."

"No!"

"They have to serve us three meals, because we're flying so far and so long."

"Is the jumbo the biggest plane in the world?"

"It was. But for some years now the Airbus 380, which has two stories, has been the biggest."

"Ours has two stories, too."

"Only in front. The Airbus 380 has two its whole length."

"Will we fly it some day?"

"Maybe. What about the games on the screen in front of you? You're not interested?"

"I'd rather look at the clouds out the window."

"Far below us."

"How high are we flying, daddy?"

"It says right here on the screen. Let me take a look." He clicks a few times and the course of the flight appears on the screen. "Thirty-three thousand feet. And you know where we're at right now?"

"No."

"Above the Black Sea."

"But I don't see it."

"Because we're above the clouds. The sea is underneath."

"Will there be clouds the whole way?"

"No, when it clears, you'll see. Perhaps then we'll be further along, and you'll see land."

"Daddy?"

"What?"

"Is it possible for the plane to fall through the clouds to the ground?"

"That hardly ever happens."

"Could it happen to us?"

"Are you afraid?"

"A little. Because then I would never see mom again."

"You'll see her, Hugo. You'll see her. That's why we're flying to Australia. Know what? I think I'll have another glass of wine."

"And I'll have juice."

***

"Daddy?"

"What, sonny?"

"Why do all of my classmates have mommies, and I don't?"

"Wait a minute... Of course, you have one."

"My classmates' mommies come for them after school and drive them home."

"Look..."

"Mine never does."

"But your dad comes. Isn't it nice that you're special and one of the few whose dad comes instead of his mom?"

"Other dads come for them, too, but not always."

"Well, I always come, and you should be proud of that."

"I can't be."

"Why not?"

"Because they ask me where my mom is. And when I say I don't know, they call me an orphan."

"Oh, Hugo…"

"And they make fun of me."

"Why don't you say that your mom is on a business trip? Didn't we agree that would be your answer?"

"I did say that a few times, but no one believed me."

"It's nobody's business where your mom is. Some children's moms have died, and they'll never see them again. Not yours. Yours is alive."

"But…"

"What?"

"Why does she live so far away?"

"That's how it turned out."

"Why?"

"Hugo, when you're a child, everything is more or less simple. When you grow up, things often get complicated. And the fact that your mom lives in Australia is, unfortunately, one of those complications."

"Will she recognize me?"

"I send her a picture of you every month."

"Really?!"

"Yes. So she sees how you're growing."

"What about me? How will I recognize her?"

"When she sees you at the airport, she'll run up, hug you, and start crying."

"Won't she be glad to see me?"

"From joy, Hugo. From happiness. Because she hasn't seen you for so long. Grown-ups often cry when they're happy.

"They cry when they're sad and cry when they're happy?"

"Grown-ups are a special kind of people. In ten or fifteen years you'll be one of them."

"And I'll cry when I'm happy?"

"Let's hope there will be many such moments. Many more than when you'll cry because you're sad."

"I wouldn't want to cry when I'm a grown up."

"Why not?"

"Because I cry too much now, when I'm small."

"You hardly ever cry, Hugo. And I have to congratulate you on that."

"I never cry during the day. Even if somebody kicks me or hurts me at school, I don't cry."

"I'm proud of you."

"I cry at night."

"At night?"

"Yes, at night, when I should be asleep, but I can't. I usually start as soon as you close my door. And I cry almost all night."

"Oh, Hugo… Why didn't you tell me?"

"Because it wouldn't help."

"How do you mean?"

"I cry because of mom. Because I'm the only one in the class without a mom."

"But… at least you could have told me."

"I would, if that would bring mom back. But it wouldn't."

"Hugo, tell me. Would you rather live with your mom or would you rather keep living with your daddy?"

"With both. That's how it used to be. Wasn't it, daddy?"

"It was, and it was nice, but nothing in this world lasts forever."

"How long ago did mom leave on her business trip?"

"Two years ago. A month before your sixth birthday."

"Why couldn't she wait so we could blow out the candles together?"

"I don't know."

"Only you were there."

"I was. And always will be. And we'll always blow out the candles on our birthdays."

"Did you hit her?"

"What?"

"Did you hit mom?"

"Hugo… Where did you get that idea?"

"Mike told me."

"Mike… in school?"

"His parents told him. That you hit mom, and so she left. And she'll never come back, because she's afraid that you'll hit her again."

"Hugo, I swear to God and by my love for you that I only hit your mom once in my life. Maybe I gave her a dirty look once in a while, but only because she deserved it."

"How?"

"Hugo… you're already sadder than most children. Please, don't force me to tell you things that would make you even sadder."

"Once you said that there's a reason for everything we do."

"There is."

"Tell me the reason I'd be even sadder if you told me what you're hiding."

"Hugo, I'm not hiding anything from you."

"Why did mom leave?"

"Hugo, I want you to remember her well. In twenty hours you'll see her, and she'll hug you and hold you tight…"

"I'm without a mom now, because you hit her. And I cry every night. That's what you wanted. Didn't you?"

"How could I do something to make you cry when I love you so much?"

"I don't know."

"Ask yourself. How could you imagine something like that? Would you like daddy to start crying?"

"You don't miss mom. I miss her."

"Hugo... I miss her, too."

"Then why don't you ask her to come home?"

"Because things aren't so simple, Hugo! Sorry, I didn't mean to yell. You just don't know how complicated grown ups' world is."

"Then I never want to grow up."

"Unfortunately, you won't be able to avoid that."

"If the plane falls through the clouds to the ground, I won't have to."

"Hugo, control yourself and believe that your mom still loves you. Just like I do. And that her being away is just something you'll have to get used to."

"I want mom to come home with us."

"I'm afraid that's a dream that won't come true. But you'll live with your mom for two weeks, and that will be enough for you until next summer."

"And then you and I will go back home?"

"That's right."

"Without mom?"

"Unfortunately."

Hugo starts to cry, barely audibly, then continues more loudly, then becomes hysterical and starts to yell for everyone in the plane to hear. All heads turn in his direction, quite a few passengers get up to see what's happening. The head steward hurries over with two flight attendants. All three look frightened.

"Is there a doctor on board?" asks dad. "He's having an attack of hysteria and needs a sedative."

"Is there a doctor on board?" the head steward hollers and looks around.

A middle aged gentleman sitting on the other side gets up, opens the luggage compartment overhead, takes out a classic physician's bag, and sets out around the restroom towards the child, who is giving the impression that he will choke from crying.

The doctor puts his bag on the floor, searches around in it, and takes out a cartridge and a needle. He handles them deftly, like doctors do, and sticks the needle into the child's thigh, right through his pants. The hysteria subsides into sobbing, which slowly fades into silence.

***

"Hugo, are you alright?"
"Was I sleeping?"
"You sure were. It's night outside."
"I'm tired."
"That's normal. Just keep sleeping."
"Was I asleep a long time?"
"Four hours."
"Why is it night outside all of a sudden?"
"When you fly east you're speeding towards night. That's because the Sun travels west—that is, because the Earth is spinning, so that... I'll explain it some other time."
"Will we be there soon?"
"I'm afraid not. We're flying over the Bay of Bengal. Across the ocean. The clouds are gone, and if you look outside, you'll see the stars above us."
"It's dark under us. I don't see the ocean."
"At night, the ocean always looks dark."
"Then how do you know we're flying over the ocean?"
"I see it on the screen. Shall I turn yours on? You'll see a map with a little picture of the plane blinking on it. And you'll know exactly where we are. Shall I turn it on?"
"No, you'll tell me."
"You'll also see other things. How high we're flying, how fast, what time it is at home and here, where we are, and where we're going."
"Is mom already waiting at the airport?"
"We still have fifteen hours to Australia."

"In this plane?"

"We'll change planes in Singapore."

"Oh, boy."

"It will pass quickly. We'll read a little, sleep a little, there will be another meal…"

"I'd rather not sleep."

"You can read. We brought two books. So far you read only one."

"Both. I read the second when you were sleeping."

"Did I sleep, too?"

"A long time. And you were snoring."

"I can't help it. Did anyone get upset?"

"No. Every time you started to snore, I nudged you a little, and you stopped."

"See how good you are."

"Daddy, why don't people look alike?"

"What do you mean?"

"Wouldn't it be funny if all the people in a plane had the same faces? If the dads were alike, and the moms, and the grandpas and grandmas, and all the children?"

"Only identical twins look alike. And there aren't many of them. There don't seem to be many on this plane."

"Maybe there is one, but we don't know, because his brother stayed home."

"You're not tired any more?"

"No, I'd like to talk."

"Then let's. Although I have to say that it's me who's tired now."

"Don't you want to talk?"

"I'm happy to, Hugo. As long as you're full of energy."

"Daddy, if people don't look like one another, does that mean there's only one of a kind in the world and each one is special?"

"Exactly. There're no two alike. Relatives resemble each other, of course, but in fact each one is different, and each one has his own life and his own story."

"Different from others?"

"Maybe not completely, but yes, different."

"Daddy, is it possible that there's another kid on the plane flying to his mom?"

"It's not impossible. And since the most unlikely things are often also the most likely, it's very possible that you're right."

"Do you think I could find him if I asked around the plane?"

"The stewardesses wouldn't allow that."

"But what if they know?"

"How would they know the stories of five hundred passengers? After all, they don't know ours."

"Too bad. Because then I could talk with him. About our moms. Why he doesn't remember his. Why I don't remember mine. And why his left."

"I'm sorry, Hugo, but that's impossible."

"Daddy, how many people are there in the world?"

"A lot. Something over seven billion."

"And every one has a story?"

"To some extent. Because many people's stories are alike in some respects. In general, not in the details."

"But I think they're very alike."

"Why do you think so?"

"Because of the books we get at the library. I read them."

"You know why I'm most proud of you, Hugo? Because you love books more than computer games."

"But you know that's not true, daddy."

"Then why haven't you played even one game on the screen in front of you since we took off? You have more than a hundred to choose from."

"Because I'm thinking about mom."

"You read two books."

"I think of mom even when I'm reading. Mom

becomes one of the characters in the book. Sometimes she's a squirrel, other times a bird or a fox. That's not possible when I play those games."

"I hope it stays that way."

"Because, daddy, I think that people's stories are really the same."

"Perhaps the authors of the books don't have enough imagination."

"No, the stories are great. I'll read both books again. Because they're really good. I'm trying to tell you something else."

"I'm listening."

"In all the books I've read, in school or at home, the same things happen"

"Is that so?"

"People or animals can't stand each other. People or animals love each other. Some work hard, others are lazy. Some lie, others tell the truth. Some are poor, others rich. Some are evil and attack others. Some defend them. Some just walk away and don't care that the ones they left suffer. Some are traitors, some steal. Some protect their friends. When I read books, daddy, it seems to me that all people in the world are alike. Daddy, are you sleeping?"

"No, I'm thinking about what you said."

"Do you think it's stupid?"

"No way. You said something that makes me think."

"Once you said that children also have the right to say something stupid. You said that's how imagination grows."

"That's right, Hugo, but what you just said is far from imagination. You said something that's true."

"Will you give me a candy?"

"Sure, Hugo. You convinced me that there aren't as many stories as people in the world. There're a certain number of stories in the world that are common to all. A half million people can have the same life story, at least in general terms. Maybe a hundred thousand children are traveling to see their moms at this minute. In planes, buses, cars, on bikes, and even on foot. And the reasons that mom left could be the same in half the cases."

"Will you give me a candy, daddy?"

Dad searches his pocket and hands Hugo two candies. "I'll give you two."

"I'll take one," says Hugo, "and the other later." He puts the candy in his mouth and starts to suck it. "Thanks, daddy."

"Welcome. You've never deserved a candy more that now."

"Why?"

"Because you opened a box in dad's brain that until now has been shut."

"We have boxes in our brains?"

"That's an expression, Hugo. These boxes are—how should I put it—awareness of the nature of the world. Of the nature of people."

"I don't understand."

"If there is only a certain number of possible relations between people and a certain number of life stories, it's very possible that all of the stories are present in the over five hundred something passengers on this plane. Each one has his own, of course, but if we count them, we could say the stories of all mankind are present in this plane on the way to Australia."

"You won't be mad if I say something?"

"No."

"I think you drank too much wine."

"On the contrary, Hugo. Too little. I'll order another glass. You? Fruit juice?"

"I'm not thirsty. Can you get the map on my screen?"

"Why?"

"So I can see how fast we're getting to mom."

***

"Daddy, why do we have to get on another plane in Singapore?"

"Because there are no direct flights from London to Australia. It's too far."

"Will that plane be as big?"

"Probably smaller."

"Why?"

"Because more people fly from London to Singapore than from Singapore to Sydney."

"Why?"

"Because, Hugo, Sydney, where mom is waiting for us, is the final stop. And Singapore is a crossroads, where people change and fly further in more than twenty directions."

"I'd like to see mom soon."

"Look, ten hours more after twenty hours and two hours at the airport isn't so bad. It's stressful, but only rockets fly faster than this plane."

"Then we'd get to the moon before Australia."

"Possibly. But your mom isn't on the Moon. It's more like your dad's on the Moon. Besides, you can buy your mom a present at the airport in Singapore."

"I don't have any money."

"You'll pick it out, and I'll pay."

"Daddy, do all boys my age have to listen to their dads?"

"Not at all, although it's not a bad thing."

"Why not?"

"Because dads have a lot of life behind them. A lot of experience. A lot of knowledge. And they know better what the results of decisions will be."

"Did you know what the result would be of mom's decision to go away and leave us at home?"

Dad is silent.

"Daddy?"

"Mom's decision wasn't mine. My decision was that you would stay with me."

"And how did mom decide? Not to take me along?"

"Look, Hugo, these things …"

"Why did she leave, daddy?"

"Would you rather live with her?"

"No, I'd like to know why she left."

"I don't want you to think badly of her. I already told you."

"But I don't. I love her. Not more than you, but just like you. Maybe a little more."

"Why?"

"Because I see you every day, because you scold me, because you don't give me enough candy, and I haven't seen mom for two years."

"Look, Hugo…"

"You hide things from me, why do you do that?"

"Believe me, Hugo, it's for your own good."

"Is there a boy my age sitting around here?" He lifts himself in his seat and looks around.

"I don't think so."

"Strange. Because I remember a little while ago a boy started yelling so loudly that his dad was embarrassed and a doctor had to rush over. He gave the boy a shot so he would fall asleep."

"What are you trying to say?"

"That can happen again."

"Hugo, are you blackmailing me?"

"Why are there tears in your eyes?"

"Are you aware that I'll have to tell you something that will make you sad? And maybe you'll hate me for it?"

"I would never hate you."

"Really?"

"I love you more than anyone in the world. Never mind what you did to mom to make her leave."

"I didn't do anything to her."

"Then why did she leave?"

"Hugo... your mom had problems. I don't know how things are now, but I'd say she still has them."

"What problems?"

"She drank. She liked things they call drugs. She was in treatment a few times. Even after you were born, she didn't change."

"Why not?"

"I don't know. Maybe I didn't help her enough."

"Why didn't you?"

"Because she wasn't true to me. Because she went out to the bars for fun, and God only knows what she did."

"Did you hate her?"

"No, Hugo, I loved her. She was different before you were born. At least it seemed that way to me."

"You loved her."

"That was the biggest problem."

"Why?"

"If you love someone, you forgive too much, hoping the person will change. You mistakenly believe that you're guilty of something or other, too."

"I always loved mom."

"Me, too, Hugo. To me, our mom will remain the most beautiful woman in the world. But that's not enough. And maybe that's exactly the problem."

"Why, daddy?"

"Because we don't know how to value what's best in people. We value what pleases the eye."

"Is my mom beautiful?"

"More than you can imagine."

"When you say that's not enough, what more would you like?"

"Faithfulness, Hugo. Trust that your mom is only yours and mine. Maybe I'm old-fashioned, but for me that's the most valuable thing. Only if I know that your mom is ours and only ours can I look you straight in the eye."

"Why did she leave?"

"She met someone. A dad of some other boy two years older than you. His mom didn't abandon him; she died very young. And your mom decided to go to Australia with the two of them."

"Without me?"

"No. She really wanted to take you with her. But I fought for you, it went to court, and there was a lot of ugliness. The court decided you would stay with me."

"Are you happy?"

"Unbelievably. I wouldn't have a life without you."

"Was the one she went to Australia with a dentist, too?"

"Not as far as I know. He works in the Sydney stock exchange."

"What's a stock exchange?"

"It's a building where a lot of money changes hands. Nowadays they'd call it a holy place. Like two thousand years ago it was called a temple."

"Does my mom like money?"

"I don't know, Hugo. I really don't know. I'd rather not think about that. Things are way more complicated. It's not only about money. It's about other things, too. Things you wouldn't understand at your age."

"Can I try harder and understand things, daddy?"

"You can't, Hugo. And thank God that's the way it is."

"Why?"

"Because every stage in life brings new understanding appropriate for your age, and that's just as it should be."

"Did she leave more because of you or because of me?"

"Not at all because of you. She misses you. She keeps writing that she'd like to see you."

"But why would she leave because of you? You're the best dad in the world."

"I think she left because of herself."

"You know what? I'll convince her to come home with us."

"That would be wonderful."

"You don't hold it against her that she left?"

"I'll be quite honest, Hugo. I hold it against her very much. But for you, I'm ready to forgive her everything. My life would be senseless without you."

"Will you be very sad if I don't become a dentist when I grow up?"

"Not in the least. But why don't you want to be a dentist?"

"Because I don't want to hurt people."

"Sometimes it's necessary in order for the pain to go away later."

"You know what I'll be when I grow up?"

"An inventor?"

"A fighter. I'll beat up anyone who makes other people sad."

"I like that. But…"

"What, daddy?"

"You'll have a lot of work."

2.

The Final Journey

The old lady spreads her gnarled fingers and places them on the hand of the gentleman about her age, maybe a little older, sitting by the window.

"What are you thinking about?"

"Oh," the gentleman wakes up, "About everything and nothing."

"Is that possible?"

"At our age, my dear, even the impossible is possible."

"And what's that?"

"That we both reach a hundred."

"I don't know if I'd like that."

"Of course not. So that I would bore you another ten years? You always knew what was good for you."

"And you've never changed."

"No?"

"At our wedding you said—do you know what you said?"

"No. And you remember something I said seventy years ago?"

"Only what you said. Nothing else."

"What did I say that was so unforgettable?"

"You said… wait, I'll remember."

"Aha… So it's not so easy."

"You said, 'If in ten years time I start to bore you, you can find someone else, I won't hold it against you.'"

"I said that?"

"You did."

"And you remember that?"

"As if you said it yesterday."

"And why do you remember that and not all the other things?"

"I remember, because after ten years of marriage you really did start to bore me."

"Why didn't you tell me?"

"It was too late. We had two children."

"All the same."

"And there was another problem."

"What?"

"I loved you."

"Oh, my dear…"

"What?"

"How could we live together so many years and raise two daughters without you telling me that I bored you?"

"It's a miracle, isn't it? Especially because I started to bore you many years before you did me."

"That's not true."

"Come on. What use is a white lie now, when we're on our final journey?"

"Our final journey?"

"Do you think we'll ever fly again?"

"You know that we won't. Not long after we arrive, we'll die."

"Surely our daughter didn't invite us in order to get rid of us!"

"She means well, but she'll soon get tired of us. Maybe we should have stayed in the rest home."

"And what would we do there?"

"We'd be bored, just like we'll be at her house. And it will be difficult to live with people we don't even know."

"Now I don't understand you."

"I was always a realist."

"Isn't it nice that at sixty years old she wants to take

care of her parents, who are at death's door?"

"Maybe she thinks we have a lot stashed away."

"We left the house to the rest home in exchange for hospice care. We scraped together just enough for the plane tickets."

"She doesn't know that."

"You've become very forgetful."

"That's a nice accusation at my age."

"Just in her last letter she wrote that she would hire an attorney to force the rest home to return us most of the money for the house."

"You know those private rest homes. They'll find something in the agreement. The case will drag on for years. We'll already be in heaven by then."

"And she'll get the money."

"I told you that she's interested in the money, not us. Although she'll have to divide it with her sister."

"Sister? She doesn't deserve anything."

"The law is the law."

"I don't know why even now you have to be like you always were."

"Boring?"

"Doubting. About your own daughter. Who lives alone on an abandoned farm and will enjoy our company."

"But we hardly know her, and she doesn't know us at all."

"How can you say something like that?"

"She visited us five times since she went to Australia thirty years ago."

"Six."

"Even if she came ten times, it was always for a few days, and years passed in between."

"She wrote."

"Cards. For Christmas, Easter, and birthdays. Yours. Never for mine."

"She must've forgotten when it is. After all, you

never even celebrated it. On purpose. You said it's a day like any other. I'm surprised you even know how old you are."

"True, maybe I mistakenly added five years and I'm actually younger."

"You and your jokes. They always aggravated me."

"You never told me that."

"There're quite a few things I didn't tell you. I wanted peace at home. But now we're on the way to heaven, now I can say everything I hushed up."

"To heaven? I didn't know that."

"Well, then to hell."

"And what did you hush up?"

"Almost everything I wanted to tell you but changed my mind at the last minute so as not to hurt you."

"But you still did. Often. Especially with your silence."

"I'm sorry. At least *you* always said it all. Without thinking you might hurt me."

"My dear, are we going to argue now, in the plane, when we haven't our entire lives?"

"I don't know. There are spaces between us that we never talked about."

"Is it necessary to talk about them?"

"Maybe not, but once in a while it's necessary to admit a few things."

"I admit that I wasn't always the best husband. But I tried."

"That at least is something."

"Obviously too little for you."

"What about me? Was I always the best wife?"

"Absolutely. Since you were the only one, I haven't had a chance to compare, but I never felt a desire to hold anything against you."

"Why are we talking about the past, when they only thing we really have is the future?"

"You started."

"That's what you always say. It's always me who started it."

"But this time you did, don't get offended. I'll just be quiet, that'll be best."

"That was always the best. You fell silent, and I simply spilled out my troubles to the walls."

"Oh, my heart aches when I hear that."

"Isn't it right that now, when our journey is nearing its end, we finally talk about certain things?"

"On the contrary. Now is the time for us to recall only beautiful things and to forget the bad ones."

"Some things can't be forgotten."

"I'm going to ask the pilot to turn the plane around. I'd like to go back to the rest home."

He starts to get up. His wife pulls him down.

"Forgive me. There's really no point in spoiling our final moments."

"You go on if you want. I'm going to take a nap."

"What do you most regret in your life?"

"In my life with you?"

"In general."

"A lot of things, most of them stupid, the mistakes of youth, male vanities and indulgences."

"You were never self-indulgent."

"Have you forgotten, or are your trying to flatter me."

"So there's nothing in your life for which you're really sorry."

"It's too late for all that, my dear, too late. The wounds have already healed, and if they haven't, what sense would there be in rubbing salt in them? What about you?"

"If I regret anything? Only one thing."

"That you married the fool sitting next to you."

"That I gave birth to our first daughter."

"Because she killed her partner with an axe?"

"Ever since then I wonder what portion of the guilt is mine."

"Why do women so like to feel guilt for things they did not do?"

"She's my child, I raised her."

"Hitler also had a mother. Is she guilty for everything he did?"

"Although I didn't raise her alone. You did your part."

"Then it's fine. I assume the guilt for her madness. I should be in jail, and she should be a lumberjack, good as she is with an axe."

"How can you just ignore something that I want to talk about?"

"Because it's too late, my dear. Do I have to repeat that to you all the way to Australia? Actually, if my memory serves me right, I've been repeating that to you half my life."

"Too bad."

"She probably doesn't know herself what went wrong in her head. After all, she was a normal woman who at a certain moment did something that she otherwise would never have done."

"She actually did have a reason…"

"Well, you see, the question is solved."

"Although the court didn't admit it."

"Can you see now how quickly an unjustified sense of guilt drives a person to the edge of madness?"

"What do you mean?"

"Her reason was jealousy. Did her partner betray her? No. They went to a restaurant, where one of the waitresses recognized him and said she hadn't seen him for a good ten years, patted his shoulder, and added he should call her sometime."

"She probably thought…"

"That he had something with the waitress ten years before?"

"That isn't out of the question…"

"And that was the reason for our daughter to go home

with her partner, promise the neighbor to cut firewood for her the next day, but because she didn't want to wake decided to take the axe that evening? Then she waited for her partner to fall asleep and smashed his skull? A thirty-five year old woman?"

"Please..."

"And then pulled the door off its hinges, ran into the wall so she was all bloody, and told the police that someone broke in and did it?"

"She was obviously horrified by what she did..."

"At least her partner couldn't be horrified, he was dead."

"You don't understand..."

"His brains were hanging out of his head, claimed a report in one of the tabloids."

"It's not that I'm trying to justify what she did. It frightens me. She had our genes."

"Yours definitely, I'm not sure about mine."

"You know what, that's going a little too far..."

"Can you swear that in all the decades of our marriage you haven't once jumped the fence?"

"You've been insulting me all my life!"

"I've been insulting *you*?"

"And this was the worst insult of all."

"I can't imagine that someone of my blood, who was normal all his life, would suddenly lose his mind at sixty-five."

"But you can imagine that happening to someone of my blood?"

"Not yours. But maybe to someone who inherited the genes of a casual stranger to whom, generous as you are, you wanted to give a little fun on his birthday. As thanks for some service. Anything is possible."

"What about you?"

"Me?"

"How many times did you jump the fence?"

"I was so awkward at the first try that I broke my legs getting over, and then I didn't dare any more."

"Ha ha."

"Even if I did, *you* gave birth to a daughter with an axe, not me."

"In short, I'm to blame."

"I'll say it again: it's too late. It's too late and senseless to regret something that happened beyond our control and that we can't change. Our journey is ending, we made some mistakes, but in general we were an ideal couple."

"I didn't know."

"I just told you."

"Why didn't you tell me before?"

"I was too busy. You were, too. And you were never sentimental. You would have laughed if I told you."

"You know, my whole life I've been asking myself what it would have been like had I married another."

"You could have done that any time, I wouldn't have prevented it."

"Do you have any idea how many times in my life your hurt me without knowing it?"

"And you? How would you feel if I told you that all my life I asked myself what my life would have been like had I married another?"

"You could have done that any time, I wouldn't have prevented it."

"And why didn't either of us do it?"

"Because we are cowards?"

"Because we love each other."

"We do?"

"More than most people."

"Most?"

"Well, I don't know about others, but the main thing is that we love each other."

"Then everything must be fine."

"It is. The only thing that bothers me is our daughter who lives alone on an abandoned farm in the middle of the Australian wilderness and plans to take care of her parents, who can barely get around."

"What bothers you?"

"What if she has the same genes as her older sister? And she invited us with an intent? And she already has a plan worked out? She also uses firewood to heat. Do you remember the pictures she sent us of the farm? I clearly recall the stacks of fat logs and an axe leaning against them."

"At least it will be quick."

"If she knows how to swing it. Otherwise it will be bad."

"Can we take a rest from analyzing family affairs?"

"I said some time ago that I'd like to take a nap."

"Why didn't you?"

"Because now that we're both senile, our conversations are a great source of fun."

"Senile? Did you know that two days before we left I solved a crossword puzzle?"

"And did you know that two days before we left I told the old age home director that she's the most obnoxious woman in the world and they won't even have her in hell?"

"Good for you."

"It's a habit. You know me."

"And where will we end up? In heaven?"

"In an urn, my dear. In an urn."

***

"I see you're in a much better mood after going to the restroom."

"What man wouldn't be?" the gentleman replies and gradually sits back down.

"Not to mention women."

"Women don't have a prostate."

"That's true. But we have a bladder that can give out."

"Thank God yours is excellent. You only went once since we left. I went eight times."

"Because you drank eight times more than me."

"If that were true, I'd be in a better mood than I am."

"And what did you find so funny?"

"When I was waiting in line, I got into a conversation with a doctor. He told me that prostate cancer progresses very slowly and takes twenty years to kill you."

"Was he drunk?"

"No."

"Or maybe you're so drunk that you misunderstood him?"

"My dear, you know very well how much I can imbibe before it has an effect. They'd never give me such quantities on a plane."

"And you simply told him that you have prostate cancer?"

"First he said that he's a doctor."

"I had to wait a year and a half before you told me what was wrong with you, and you tell a stranger right at the restroom door?"

"Why should I hide something that can't concern him? With you it was different, I didn't want to worry you."

"It hurt me that you didn't tell me right away when you found out."

"That's how you women are. You're not interested in the heart of the matter. First and foremost you're offended."

"If I were to add up how many times in our lives either of us was offended, I would be far behind you."

"I am never offended, I just get angry."

"Which men see as a more noble thing."

"Can we stop?"

"What?"

"The stupid jabs? Which we don't mean?"

"Haven't we been doing that our whole life?"

"True. And it was fun."

"But now we're on our final journey. You forgot to tell the doctor by the restroom door that your cancer has metastasized."

"It has?"

"It has, my dear. To the liver, pancreas, lungs, and stomach."

"Then twenty more years is out of the question."

"I'm afraid so."

"Well, then two years. Ten percent. An eternity."

"No doubt the moment when the jabs have to end and we'll have to ask ourselves what in fact we got out of life."

"Memories of already departed friends torment me more that the thought of my own death. They did it like secretly, without informing me about it."

"Should they have?"

"Probably not. We invite each other to weddings, anniversaries, and birthdays. Never to a burial."

"The time will come for that, too."

"You won't believe it, but I've been aware of my generation passing away for ten years already. At every friend's death it seems a piece of me has been lost."

"And it has."

"When we pass away, there will no longer be anyone like us in the world. Each of us is a unique."

"Small comfort."

"Look around the plane. If we go down, it won't be five hundred people that'll die, but five hundred different people."

"Are you sure?"

"Completely. When people die, they leave behind holes that can't be filled. Our genetic fate is that each of us is unrepeatable. An individual who has to find his way in life, live his own way, and die that way."

"Are you afraid?"

"I'd be lying if I said I'm not."

"Me, too, my love. I'm afraid, too."

"But the strongest feeling inside me is gratitude. I loved and was loved. At twenty-five, that would have seemed syrupy to me, but young people are allowed to make fun of older people's feelings. After all, they don't know what awaits them."

"Let the young have their youth and live with the illusions that we have lived with."

"I'm comforted by having given and received a lot in life. For a short time, I was a wondrous thinking animal on a wondrous planet, maybe the only one like it in the boundless universe; on the other hand, it was long enough to start to bore me."

"Along with me?"

"No, my love. You were and remain my only reward."

"Don't we always get what we deserve?"

"That would mean that God and the world are just, and that God didn't slip up. You know very well that it's a matter of coincidence. In our case, things turned out rather for the better than worse. We have to be grateful for that."

"I am."

"I'm trying to be."

"You don't have much time."

"I know. But you're fine. Women live five years longer than men. Who knows why."

"Is that what you wish me? Five years without you before they take me away as well?"

"My love, when the time comes, I can't take you with me. And that can happen days after we get to our daughter's."

"It could turn out that I die before you."

"Impossible."

"What if I, too, have an illness I didn't tell you about, because I didn't want to upset you?"

38

The gentleman is silent for a while. "You're joking."

"What if I'm not?"

"What illness?"

"Fear that you'll die before me and I'll be bored without you?"

"Did you know that I've been living with that fear for some years now?"

"Then the only solution is for us to go together."

"Together?"

"At the same time. Let's say the plane plunges into the ocean."

"Do we have the right to take with us so many people we don't even know?"

"No."

"On the other hand, life is full of almost unbelievable coincidences."

"Well, now we're on your favorite subject. Probability."

"Don't you think it's interesting?"

"You've told me many things, but since I immediately forget everything, it will be new to me."

"How likely is it that you go to the Ghanaian embassy in Ouagadougou for a visa and there run into a classmate you haven't seen since graduation?"

"Barely if at all."

"And how likely is it that after all those long years the classmate recognizes you and invites you to visit him when you get to Ghana?"

"A little more."

"And how likely is it that just then you come down with malaria and the classmate takes care of you a good three weeks, feeding and comforting you, and taking you from doctor to doctor?"

"Most improbable."

"But as you well know, all that happened."

"When something unlikely happens, it becomes likely. Even more, it becomes a fact."

"How likely is it that two passengers on this plane have identical suitcases and after landing will take the wrong one from the conveyor belt?"

"Very likely. That happens all the time."

"And how likely is it that one of them has a tag on his suitcase with the hotel address and his cell phone number?"

"Less likely, but still possible. That happened to us on the flight to Egypt."

"Let's forget the facts and stick with the realm of probability. How likely is it that at customs, when you exit, they open a suitcase that looks like your but isn't and find five packages of heroine in it? And you can't prove that the suitcase isn't yours? And you go to jail for thirty years, or they shoot you, as happens in some places."

"It's possible but hardly likely."

"But that happened, too."

"And it happened that instead of nothing it is the world that exists. Which is the most unlikely thing of all."

"Although you just said that the unlikely after it happens becomes not only likely but a fact."

"And the world is a fact. Although there's the same possibility that it would not exist. It was too unlikely. But now that it does, it's likely."

"What law says that the female cousin of a Lebanese friend I studied with in London many years before, when she was still a kid, discovers me on a burning African road and packs me into her car?"

"Did that really happen?"

"Yes. Where does coincidence end and fate begin?"

"At the same point?"

"How likely is it that my acquaintance from South Africa suddenly realizes on a London bus that sitting next to him is his uncle from America who by pure coincidence decided to visit the city at the same time as him?"

"You never told me that."

"No?"

"At least I don't remember."

"I think I've told you that five times already."

"One more proof that I'm closer to dementia than you."

"My love, if one of us is demented, it's me. I could ask you how likely it is that a ninety-two year old will manifest signs of dementia."

"More than likely."

"Then why get upset? The dementia will disappear along with us."

"And what will be left?"

"Nothing. That's not only likely, but a fact."

"And what if we land up in hell?"

"Let's go back to the uncle from America with whom my acquaintance unexpectedly found himself on a London bus."

"In this case, probability blends with miracle."

"The likelihood of them finding themselves next to each other was no less, but no greater, in the cases of all the other people in the bus. Before chance brought them together, it was just as unlikely that X would sit next to Y as it was that my acquaintance would sit down by his uncle. According to the laws of probability, they, too, were just X and Y, with the difference that they were related. But their being relatives had nothing to do with them finding themselves next to each other in the same bus."

"It's too late for my greatest desire to come true."

"Which is?"

"To understand everything you try to tell me."

"There's nothing to understand. Every day a million highly unlikely things happen, and we don't realize at all how unlikely they were until coincidence allowed them to happen. We only realize their degree of unlikelihood when during some event they overwhelm us with wonder. Our understanding of probability is illogical and emotional."

"I wonder how likely you'll find a circumstance I haven't mentioned to you because I didn't want to put you in a bad mood."

"Let me tell you one more thing. May I?"

"You always could."

"Let's say you're ninety years old."

"Ninety-two."

"Let's say, I said."

"Right."

"And you have a house but no money for a normal life. And let's say I'm forty-seven."

"As you once were."

"And you, being clever, offer the following agreement: You'll sell me the house on the condition that you can stay in it until you die, and I pay you five hundred pounds a month in support. When you die, the house is mine."

"That's an expensive deal."

"For whom?"

"For you."

"Because it's more than likely that you will die in a few years?"

"Exactly."

"It doesn't seem at all likely that I would have to support you longer than we both expect?"

"Absolutely unlikely."

"Fifty years ago a certain French lady made such an agreement with a lawyer. He was convinced that the woman was stupid. He didn't know that someone who reaches ninety on average can expect to live another six."

"He thought she would die at ninety-two."

"That seemed to him more than likely."

"But is it?"

"Ten years later she celebrated her centenary. Still in her house. Statistically speaking, she could have expected another two years of life. The lawyer had to keep paying her support, although he had not only bought her house, but even overpaid."

"And two years later she finally died."

"She died when she was 122. The lawyer died two years before her."

"I would say that's unlikely."

"Everyone would, but it happened."

"What are you trying to tell me?"

"That what seems unlikely to us is often not only possible but even decided. That a hidden order rules in the chaos of life and in a world that is chaos, and permits rare events to be possible."

"As long as we're on probability, can I also ask something?"

"Be my guest."

"How likely is it that in about one year we will both die?"

"That would be wonderful. Then we would avoid complaining, loneliness, and missing the one who died first. But it's unlikely."

"Why?"

"Because I don't want it to happen. Because I'd like you to live another ten years."

"Without you?"

"Our older daughter will get out of jail in five years, and you'll be enjoying the intellectual poverty of our other daughter's company on a farm in Australia."

"Even now you can be nasty."

"Just to the point, my love. I have never been nasty."

"Actually I won't miss you."

"You won't?"

"No."

"Well, you don't really have a reason to. I was a burden to you. You'll feel great relief when I kick the bucket."

"I wasn't open with you either."

"Look, we're on our final journey, we had a beautiful life, at least as compared with most people on the planet. Why should we ruin these moments with admissions of things that happened God knows how many years ago? Some secrets can go to the grave."

"I should have told you that I'm sick, too."

"Of course you are. Arthritis, varicose veins, arrhythmia, migraines. Things pile up over the years."

"Especially migraines."

"That's true, lately, especially migraines."

"Which aren't migraines, my love, but a malignant brain tumor."

A brief silence. The gentleman slowly places his left hand on the right of the lady next to him and presses it.

"I know, my love."

"How?"

"Our doctor told me. Not intentionally. He was sure I knew. It seemed unlikely to him that a wife would hide a brain tumor from her husband. And that operating was out of the question, because she wouldn't survive it."

"So we're back at probability."

"As always."

"Forgive me."

"You hid it for the same reason I did. I understand you completely."

"You pretended you didn't know, although you did the whole time. How could you?"

"At our age some things are awakened that didn't have a chance to flower—for example, acting talent."

"We lived the last year in a lie."

"Not in a lie, my love. In love. In the truest love."

"You know what I want most of all? To crash."

"Maybe we will."

"Shall we take a little nap holding hands?"

"Let's. A little practice for what awaits us can't hurt."

"What awaits us will be different from napping."
"Let's pretend it won't."

3.

Therapy

"Excuse me, ma'am," says the gentleman in a pin-striped suit, "I don't want to disturb you, but... are you o.k.?"

"Why?" starts the lady in a blue jacket sitting next to him.

"You're pale."

"No I'm not, it's makeup."

"Just a minute, I'll change my glasses." He takes off his glasses, shoves them in his left breast pocket, pulls another pair from his right, and puts them on. He leans over to the lady and looks at her closely. "That's possible, but you're pale beneath the makeup."

"And why does that concern you?"

"Because I'm all but convinced you're suffering from aerophobia."

"What's that?"

"Fear of flying."

"I don't know why that should be your problem."

"The problem is yours, ma'am. I just help people in trouble."

"I'm not in trouble and don't need any help."

"Actually it's my profession."

"Helping people in trouble?"

"I have a private practice and cure all sorts of phobias. Aerophobia, agoraphobia, arachnophobia, claustrophobia, triskaidekophobia misophobia, glossophobia, nyctophobia, ophidiophobia…

"Please stop."

"There's even a fear of knowing how many phobias there are."

"Do I also have that?"

"Clearly. Or you don't know what all those foreign words mean."

"I really don't."

"Fear of foreign words. You're completely paralyzed."

"But I took a sedative. A double dose."

"Sedatives don't help. Unless you take so much that you're out for twenty hours."

"What does help?"

"Statistics."

"I don't understand."

"Permit me to ask whether you have a driver's license."

"Of course. I drive to work. An hour there and an hour back."

"You're not afraid of traffic?"

"Not at all."

"But you should be."

"Why?"

"Because the number of deaths on the highway relative to the number of dead in plane crashes is so disproportionate that people should be shaking in terror behind the wheel."

"Oh, come on."

"In the U.S., for example, there were five million traffic accidents in 2008 alone, and only twenty plane crashes. Only twenty, ma'am."

"But when a plane crashes, everyone dies; on the roads, there are mostly just injuries."

"A lot of people survive plane crashes, too."

"No one thinks about that when they're driving."

"Then why are you afraid of flying?"

"Because I can't help it."

"The chance of dying in a traffic accident is one in ninety-eight. The chance of ending your life in a plane crash is an unbelievable one in 7,000! That means you're safest in the air."

"The problem is that I can't believe it."

"You feel safe behind the wheel, because you think you're in control. You hold the wheel and so you think you also hold your fate in your hands."

"But the wheel is in my hands. I control my driving, I make decisions. But here someone I don't know at all is sitting in the cockpit."

"And on the road? Do you know the people driving alongside you? Or the ones racing towards you?"

"Even so…"

"Don't you read newspapers?"

"I do."

"Then you know that not long ago some young German pilot intentionally flew a plane full of vacationers into an Alpine mountainside. He could have hung himself at home or jumped off a cliff, but no, he wanted to take three hundred others with him."

"I know."

"That same day, ten thousand people around the world died in traffic accidents. Is anyone excited about that?"

"You know what, after this conversation I'll have to take some more pills." She begins searching her bag. "Can you order me a glass of water?"

"We haven't even started."

"What?"

"Therapy, ma'am."

"Here, twelve kilometers above the Earth, you want to cure me of my fear of flying?"

"Phobias are most easily cured by confronting what causes the fear."

"Meaning?"

"That you inflate the fear. Like a balloon. Until it bursts."

"Are you going to do that?"

"I'll enumerate for you all the crashes that the plane we're flying in has experienced until now. In the past forty years, Boeing 747-400 has had only thirty catastrophic crashes."

"Are you joking?"

"That's exceptionally few, fewer than one a year."

"Exceptionally few?"

"Few considering that 1,514 of them have been built so far, that every day 1,200 of them fly, and that at any moment there are about 700 of them in the air."

"There are 700 of these planes in the air at this moment?"

"And since less than one a year crashes, the chances of it being precisely our plane, precisely today, are, we might say, zero."

"I can't believe it."

"The worst crash took place in 1977 on the Canary Islands, when a Dutch 747 decided to take off before receiving air controllers' permission. At that moment, invisible in the fog, an American Pan Am 747 crossed the takeoff path."

"And?"

"583 people died in the collision."

"Jesus!"

"But it wasn't in the air but on the ground. Most catastrophes take place during take off, or landing, or in the air, when a plane suddenly breaks into pieces."

"That's fine comfort!"

"In 1985, an Air India 747 on a flight from Canada to Bombay plunged into the sea near the Irish coast and killed 330 passengers. A bomb exploded onboard."

"Can that happen to us?"

"Since 2001, safety inspections at airports have become very thorough."

"I don't feel well."

"It also happens that something goes wrong with a plane for technical reasons. In 1989, a Japanese 747 experienced sudden decompression, which damaged the hydraulic system. The damage made it impossible to control the plane. The plane plunged into Mount Ugura and all 520 passengers died, along with the crew."

"Sir, not to offend you... is this the way you cure people of fear of flying?"

"It's the most effective way."

"You mean that what you're doing is therapy?"

"An attempt at therapy."

"On whom does its success depend?"

"On you, ma'am."

"Great."

"Let's consider the number of airplane crashes since the beginning. That was in 1919."

"Were there already planes then?"

"In almost a hundred years of air travel, there were only 1,062 catastrophic plane crashes."

"Only?!"

"And in ninety-six years, thirteen a year only eight times."

"And the most?"

"Twenty-four in 2011. On average it's eleven planes a year. Hardly worth mentioning."

"I don't feel at all well."

"Psychologically or physically?"

"Both."

"Glass of wine?"

"Whiskey. A double."

"I'll also have a double."

***

"Tell me some more about the phobias you cure. I think the whiskey gave me courage."

"Ma'am, your chief phobia is fear of flying. We have an opportunity to cure it."

"For good?"

"What else?"

"You're that confident in your ability?"

"A therapist who doesn't believe in himself isn't worth the title."

"True. Maybe the extra pills I took helped more than the whiskey."

"But the path to a cure is complicated."

"Why?"

"The opposite effect is possible—that afterwards you'll have an even greater fear of flying."

"I feel quite fine now."

"That's called apathy. Fear of flying is cured when you get on a plane with the full knowledge that you can die at any moment, and at the same time fully believing that something like that can never happen."

"How can I believe that this cannot happen when I know that it can?"

"Did you know that most fatal accidents happen at home, in the apartments and houses where people live?"

"No."

"People slip in the bathroom, fall off ladders, are electrocuted repairing an outlet, fall down the stairs—there are more than a thousand causes."

"I don't think about that at home."

"Then why do you think a plane might go down when you're on it?"

"Because I'm home almost every day, but hardly ever on a plane."

"You feel safe at home, because almost nothing ever happens to you. But just once or twice a year you see a report about a plane crash on TV and you get the sense that it's dangerous to fly."

"You said you would cure me."

"The first part of therapy is being introduced to situations in which planes didn't crash but simply disappeared."

"How did they disappear?"

"Vanished. Never to be found."

"Is that possible?"

"You're not acquainted with the most recent example? When Malaysian flight MH370, a Boeing 777, flying from Kuala Lumpur to Beijing mysteriously disappeared?"

"Where?"

"En route to Beijing, going more or less north, it turned left before the Thai border and flew west across northern Malaysia, then turned south and flew across the Indian Ocean until it disappeared from radar."

"It just disappeared?"

"Literally. The crew didn't send a single message about anything being wrong. They suspect it plunged into the southern Indian Ocean west of Australia."

"An unusual route to Beijing."

"Very. The pilot could have changed course only on purpose or under threat."

"By whom?"

"Would-be hijackers."

"Is there a chance of someone hijacking our plane?"

"If you look at the map on the screen, you'll see that for now we're on the anticipated course."

"But…"

"They have been searching for remains in the depths of the Indian Ocean for more than a year. Not long ago they found a piece that seemed to be a part of the plane washed up on the French island of Reunion in the southern Indian Ocean."

"And?"

"It seems that there's some strange, dirty plot behind it all."

"Is that possible?"

"Anything is possible. If we go back into the past, in 1956, an American Boeing B4 Stratojet bomber disappeared without a trace on a flight from Florida to an American base in Morocco. It was carrying two atomic bombs. They never found them."

"Oh, my God!"

"I won't enumerate all the mysterious disappearances, because it would take too long. I'll only name the most unusual ones."

"Better less than more."

"Ten years ago Greek controllers lost touch with the crew of a Helios Airways plane on a short flight from Cyprus when it began to descend towards the Athens airport. What was unusual was that the plane remained in its anticipated landing position for more than half an hour. When military jets took off to find out what was happening, they discovered the pilot incapacitated, slumped over the steerage. A half hour later the plane smashed into the side of a mountain near Athens, killing 121 people. They suspect that the air pressure in the plane gradually dropped, making landing impossible."

"Can we take a short break?"

"No, because then the therapy won't work."

"Oh…"

"Your probably know that Amelia Earhart, who in 1935 wanted to round the world in a Lockheed Electra, disappeared without a trace in the Pacific Ocean. Some say the Japanese shot her down as a suspected spy; others that she faked her death; yet others that creatures from the outer space abducted her."

"Might we not take a break?"

"No. Now comes the main blow, which might cure you. Are you brave enough?"

"I don't know."

"Have you heard of the Bermuda Triangle?"

"Who hasn't?"

"In 1945, an Avenger Torpedo bomber with a U.S. Air Force crew of thirteen disappeared there. The Americans sent a Mariner water plane with another crew of thirteen to look for the missing plane. They didn't find it. What's more, the water plane and its crew also disappeared without a trace. Even now, no one knows what happened."

"Hardly believable."

"In 1948, a flight from the Azores to Bermuda disappeared with a trace or cause in the triangle. The same year, a DC-3 en route from Puerto Rico to Miami mysteriously disappeared. A year later, a flight from Bermuda to Kingston, Jamaica disappeared in more or less the same location. And what's even more unusual, many ships also mysteriously disappeared in the area, even more than planes."

"Why?"

"There're countless theories. Everything from military conspiracies to extraterrestrials, who are supposed to have designed the Bermuda Triangle as a trap."

"And where is the triangle?"

"Far from here, ma'am, very far. It stretches from Bermuda to Puerto Rico, and Miami."

"Then we're safe."

"Completely. The only thing that bothers me a little is the number 191."

"What's wrong with that number?"

"Just like in some hotels you won't find a thirteenth floor or a room 13, you won't find flights ending in 191 with some airlines."

"Why?"

"Because people are superstitious. From 1960 until now, five flights containing the number 191 have ended in catastrophe."

"That's impossible."

"That's a fact, ma'am. And some of the worst plane crashes in American history are among them, like American Airlines flight 191. 237 people died in the crash."

"Oh, my God."

"And not long ago, three years ago, a JetBlue flight #191 pilot went mad. The co-pilot managed to shove him out of the cabin, and they got him under control with the passengers' help. He ended up in a psychiatric hospital, where he remains."

The lady crosses herself.

"What about triskaidekaphobia. Do you suffer from that?"

"I don't know."

"It's fear of the number thirteen. He probably hasn't escaped you that we're sitting in row 13."

"Really? I don't like that."

"Do you think that because of that there's an increased possibility of the plane crashing?"

"Probably not. But it's hard to shake the anxiety."

"Some airlines don't have a row 13. But Singapore doesn't pay attention to that."

"But they don't have a flight 191."

"They actually do. As I said, that's the one thing that even makes me uncomfortable."

"Why?"

"Because our flight number is 2191. Check your ticket."

"No!"

"Are you alright, ma'am? You're pale again."

"You're torturing me. Stewardess!"

"Ma'am…"

"Not another word! You're not a therapist. What a lie! You're a sadist."

"Ma'am…"

"Don't 'ma'am' me. Stewardess, please change my

seat. My neighbor has been psychologically torturing me several hours. Any more, and I'll have a stroke. Please, I *demand* you change my seat."

"I'll see what I can do."

"Just do it, otherwise you'll be responsible for my death!"

"Sir?" the stewardess turns to the phobia doctor.

"The lady is afraid of flying. We had a mutual agreement that I would try to cure her. Unfortunately, it didn't work. It will be better for me, too, if you change her seat."

"I'll see what I can do," says the stewardess.

"Please," the lady says again.

"As soon as possible," adds the therapist.

***

"Why did they move you?" the younger lady asks the older one in a blue jacket.

"The gentleman sitting next to me wouldn't leave me alone."

"Was he coming on to you?"

"If only he was! At least then I'd have a reason to smack him. No, he was describing plane crashes to me in detail."

"Nice of him."

"The last thing he said was that our plane is going to go down because the flight number ends in 191."

"He's obviously superstitious."

"And he couldn't help but mention that we were sitting in row 13"

"It won't happen."

"We really were sitting in the thirteenth row."

"The thirteenth row is up ahead, in first class. The row number you were sitting in is 31. He apparently switched the numbers."

"The jerk!"
"Are you afraid of the number thirteen?"
"Not in the least."
"I believe you. Otherwise you wouldn't have chosen to fly today."
"Why not?"
"It's the thirteenth."
"Today is the thirteenth?!"
"You didn't know?"
"My niece made the reservation. I didn't give it a thought…"
"You obviously are superstitious. At least as far as the number thirteen."
"Why?"
"Otherwise you wouldn't have taken such a deep breath."
"Am I pale?"
"I don't think any more than I am."
"Are you also afraid of flying?"
"Not overly. A low-level feeling of stress, that's all."
"That's just what I have. I put away the thought that I'm flying. I imagine I'm somewhere else, in a bus or a train."
"Then you're main fear is the number thirteen."
"Is it true that in some hotels there's no thirteenth floor?"
"You're tormenter probably told you that."
"No, I read it somewhere."
"It would amaze you how many superstitions there are in the world in this rational age."
"Do you know about those things?"
"Have you ever been in the Hotel Savoy in London?"
"It's probably very expensive."
"It's most famous for it's meter-tall black cat named Caspar."
"A meter tall!"

"Carved from wood, of course. If you're interested, I can tell you the whole story."

"Please!"

"The whole thing started more than a hundred years ago. Some businessman named Joel Woolf reserved a table for fourteen in the hotel restaurant, which even then was famous for its excellent food. At the last moment, one of the guests cancelled, and there were thirteen of them left."

"Was the number thirteen unlucky even a hundred years ago?"

"Ma'am, superstitions go back to the beginning of mankind."

"Well, it's not like I thought it started with me, but…"

"Woolf decided to ignore the old woman's tale and went ahead with the dinner. Two weeks later he was murdered in South Africa in unusual circumstances."

"Jesus!"

"After that event, the Hotel Savoy no longer permitted dinners for thirteen people. If a party of thirteen would show up, one of the servers always ate with them."

"Nice of them."

"But in 1920, they became tired of it. They ordered a woodcarver to make a replacement for the human talisman. And that's how Caspar, the black wooden cat, came to be."

"Have you ever seen it?"

"Yes. It's a marvelous art deco piece. Since then, Caspar has had dinner with all the parties that happened to be of thirteen. Every time, they would tie a napkin around his neck and serve him the same food as everyone else."

"Can you believe it!"

"During WW II, a group of revelers got so drunk at the Savoy that they stole Caspar."

"Oh, no."

"And who took care of returning him to his proper place? None other than Winston Churchill."

"Was he also afraid of the number thirteen?"

"I doubt it. It had to do with something else. But let's leave it at that."

"Then I probably don't have to be ashamed of being stressed by the number thirteen."

"Do you know where fear of the number thirteen actually comes from?"

"No."

"You don't know but you're still afraid?"

"Unfortunately."

"The number thirteen was unlucky because there were thirteen people at Jesus's last supper."

"But I'm an atheist."

"No you aren't. You've replaced faith with superstition, which is more powerful than faith and prevails over a larger part of the world than all faiths combined."

"How do you know?"

"I'm writing a dissertation. On superstitions."

"And then what will you be? A doctor of superstitions?"

"Anthropology."

"Interesting."

"Tell me, if you were going to move, and you found a beautiful and affordable house with the address 13, would you buy it?"

"Maybe. But I would be hesitant."

"And how would you feel in it?"

"Stressed. It would be hard to fall asleep."

"Then you won't be surprised that the words for death and four in Chinese and Japanese are pronounced about the same, on account of which many Chinese hospitals don't have a fourth floor. And many Japanese don't like to leave on a trip on the fourth of the month."

"Interesting."

"All this has reached California, where Chinese and Japanese restaurants' telephone numbers are half as likely to have the number four in them than other restaurants."

"My God."

"Which led a colleague of mine at the university to ask whether the fourth of the month also influences health. Is it possible that it's connected with the number of heart attacks?"

"Is it?"

"He looked at mortality data on forty-seven million people who died in America between 1973 and 1998. He compared the data on Chinese- and Japanese-Americans with data on all other Americans in the same period. And what did he find? That thirteen percent more Chinese and Japanese died on the fourth of the month."

"Good thing I wasn't born on the fourth."

"When were you?"

"I hardly dare say."

"The thirteenth?"

"Unfortunately. And it was a Friday."

"You were born on Friday the thirteenth?"

"And you've reminded me that today is the thirteenth."

"Not only the thirteenth. It's Friday."

"Oh, my God."

"One of my colleagues did a study on how many more people die in traffic accidents on Friday the thirteenth than on other days. He found it is over fifty percent."

"That means that I'll die today?"

"I understand your fear. Some years ago, the Finns did a study on how many more people than usual die on Friday the thirteenth. They found that it's thirty-two percent more women by comparison, and somewhat less in the case of men."

"Today is clearly my last day."

"I wouldn't say so. Because then it would also be the last day for more than 500 people who weren't born on Friday the thirteenth."

"I think I need a glass of wine."

"Of course. I'll call the flight attendant. I don't drink."

"Maybe I shouldn't have insisted that they move me... flight attendant?"

"Yes, ma'am."

"Can you move me back to where I was sitting before?"

"Unfortunately that won't work, ma'am."

"Why not? Look at my boarding pass. Row 31, seat D. I'm entitled to that seat."

"You said that the gentleman was disturbing you."

"All the same, I'd like to go back. Or anywhere else."

"There are no empty seats. What's bothering you?"

"Nothing. The lady is very nice."

"Then enjoy the conversation."

"Please..."

But the stewardess is gone.

"Ma'am, if anything is bothering you, I can be quiet."

"No, no, it's all very interesting..."

"One of my colleagues at the university did a study on to what extent death dates are related to birth dates. He analyzed three million California death certificates and found that women most often die within a week of their birth dates, and men a week before."

"Why the difference?"

"Women see their birthday as a chance to celebrate and they're happy about it. Men are anxious: it's one more step to the end, and they're aware of how little they've achieved in life, all of which fills them with anxiety and stress."

"I don't discount that, but I can't believe it."

"That's science, ma'am."

"I imagined science to be something completely different."

"Some very successful people were born on Friday

the thirteenth. Margaret Thatcher, Fidel Castro, and Samuel Beckett. Napoleon, for example, greatly feared the number thirteen."

"Why do you deal with these things at the university?"

"Because superstition, due to how widespread it is, influences a number of things in life: the price of homes, the number of traffic accidents, the number of deaths in a given period, the number of abortions, and other things."

"The number of abortions?"

"I can tell you something that will make you shiver."

"Oh, God, better not."

"You probably know that every year in the Chinese-Japanese almanac has a name. This is the year of the goat. Every sixty years it is the year of the fiery horse, which is the most dangerous, because it brings many bad things, especially for women. Ones born in that year have a fiery, wild temperament, which is the reason that in most cases they can't find a husband and remain single."

"That's unfair. After all, people can't choose the year they're born."

"But parents can choose a birth year. My Japanese colleague at the university found that in the last year of the fiery horse, 1966, the number of births in Japan fell by a fourth. At the same time, the number of abortions increased by twenty thousand."

"That's abnormal."

"It gets even worse. Since the year of the fiery horse is especially unfavorable to women, you would think that parents in most cases would try to get rid of girls. In 1966, it was still not possible to determine a child's sex before birth, but despite this my colleague discovered that female infant mortality was twice as high as with males."

"But... that means..."

"That parents murdered many newborn girls."

"Isn't that a crime?"

"Hard to prove."

"They also deal with that at the university?"

"Yes."

"And what are you going to do in Singapore?"

"From there I fly to Papua New Guinea. To little known tribes in the mountains. I plan to study their forms of superstition."

"But those are wild tribes."

"There're quite a few who have never seen a white person."

"Aren't you afraid?"

"To be honest, I'm more afraid that our plane will crash than I am of the wild tribes."

"Why?"

"It's a feeling, ma'am. A feeling."

"I have the same feeling. Probably a lot of passengers have it. And the flight attendants. Look, they all have worried faces. Something must be wrong."

"Although the flight is very peaceful. But we can fly into a terrible storm at any moment."

"Do you know how to pray?"

"Unfortunately not."

"I will, if you'll permit me. For the two of us. It won't bother you, will it?"

"Praying out loud?"

"That's best, don't you think?"

"That could bother some passengers. But try."

"I'd rather do it quietly. I don't want arguments about God. But if everyone on the plane believes and would pray together, then the plane would land safely."

"Unless God has decided differently."

"And you?"

"I'll nap a little, if you don't mind."

4.

Journey into Silence

"And so you say you're always on the road," says a busty, early middle-aged blonde lady. "From place to place, country to country."

"More or less," nods the handsome, slightly dour young man sitting next to her.

"Aren't you ever tempted to stay in one place? For a month or two?"

"Where, for example?"

"In some village or town."

"And what would I do there? Watch TV?"

"I like to travel, too, and to be honest, I travel a lot. But I can't imagine not having a home, some place I can escape when the world starts to exhaust me."

"How many days a year do you travel?"

"Two or three months."

"Then you spend most of the time in a refuge, not on the road."

"I need both."

"Especially a house, if most of the time you're at home."

"That's just what seems unusual about you. That you don't need a house."

"The world is my house, my purpose is movement."

"Have you ever thought of the possibility that you're not a traveler, but a person on the run?"

"From what?"

"From yourself?"

"I think I'm both."

"A traveler by dint of circumstances and a person on the run who's afraid of something?"

"Who isn't? Except you, perhaps?"

"I'm also afraid of some things, but most of all I'm afraid of turning my life into an escape."

"I'm afraid of responsibility."

"Responsibility for what?"

"Responsibility itself."

"Responsibility is always concrete."

"It depends on how you experience it. A bunch of responsibilities can change into Responsibility with a capital letter."

"Oh, really?"

"Then into something that crams us into prison and robs us of life."

"I don't understand."

"Isn't the first impression of the word 'responsibility' unpleasant?"

"For sure."

"Doesn't it ignite a fear of not carrying out the responsibility or at least not like you should?"

"An anxious feeling, but not fear."

"With responsibility comes a feeling of coercion. A feeling of something opposing a natural inclination simply to be, to release ourselves to searching for comfort and satisfaction."

"I can't agree with that. It's true that the world, including our inner one, is set up so that a greater or lesser gap exists between desire and its realization, but it's possible to bridge that gap with a combination of skill and effort."

"Which means that we can't allow ourselves to go with the flow, but have to fulfill our responsibilities?"

"No. We must live sensibly and skillfully, being prepared for defeat as well."

"The word 'must' sounded loudest."

"Forget that besides desire, fate also plays an important role in realizing desires."

"Or luck, as we say."

"If it doesn't favor us enough, and it's hard to say that it does, then we must reconcile ourselves to not being exceptional."

"Which then compels us to what? A feeling of responsibility."

"For what?"

"On the one hand, we feel responsible for achieving as many of our goals as possible; on the other we try to avoid disappointment by not expecting too much. That's how responsibility clamps the handcuffs on us."

"It only seems that way."

"Really? I know people for whom responsibility is like breathing. And others who think up responsibilities so as to have guideposts on the unmarked path through the emptiness of time. Mostly I know people who would like to avoid responsibilities but don't dare, because they think they would sabotage their goals, disappoint their parents, their friends, and themselves. Isn't that you?"

"I experience life as an opportunity, not a responsibility."

"You're blessed. When I'm calm, I often have the misfortune of doing the most basic things only because I feel I must. And I take ten steps back to gather enough drive to push myself one step ahead."

"Does it have to be that way?"

"I don't know. I have to get up, wash and shave; I have to stand in line in stores, walk in the rain in soaked shoes; I have to wander the bureaucratic labyrinths of insurance offices, embassies, municipal buildings, district offices, and political, cultural, and social organizations; I have to practice responsible patience; I have to be serious and at the same time take everything with a healthy dose of humor; I have to trust others, but not blindly, which means that I also have to doubt them and at the same time know when one and when the other; I have to be happy when there's reason enough, and even if there's no reason; I have to wait and wait for most of what a person would want to happen the same day; in short, I have to live with the feeling that responsibility comprises most of life, even the moments when we feel we have to avoid responsibilities and do just what pleases us. This means that I also have to have fun with responsibilities. I don't have the responsibility to carry out responsibilities, but sometimes to live without responsibilities."

"We have to reconcile ourselves to the facts."

"If we do, then we've admitted that we live because we must live, not because we love life. But if we insist we love life, that means we'd rather live than die."

"Oh, come on..."

"Fear of the end dictates a responsibility to live. And that responsibility dictates to us all the major and minor responsibilities, because of which our lives are such a logical series of assassination attempts on the person in us that likes to play."

"And doesn't give a damn about responsibilities."

"Especially responsibilities."

"It's impossible to live like that."

"I'm trying."

"Successfully?"

"More or less."

"By being always on the road, without knowing where to and why? Staying in strange, impersonal hotels that you can leave as soon as an impulse drives you on?"

"Something like that."

"I can't believe that's your real motive. You use the word 'responsibility' for things that have more suitable names."

"That's not true. There are responsibilities we shoulder ourselves, because we'd like to be attractive or successful. Then there are those that others burden us with, or are thrust upon us by the imperatives of survival."

"Examples, please."

"The first kind of responsibility is, for instance, a decision to lose weight."

"A decision isn't a responsibility."

"A decision becomes a responsibility as soon as we take it. An example of the second kind is obedience. When, let's say, you're making spaghetti, and your husband or wife makes you run to the store for tomato sauce."

"I would call that complying in the interests of a common goal, a good dinner."

"The third kind of responsibility is being aware of having to be pleasant with people on whom for some reason we depend."

"But not with those who depend on us in some way?"

"That too. Some responsibilities fall into all three categories—let's say, the responsibility to drive on the right side of the road and not down the middle."

"That's not a responsibility. That's common sense."

"Different categories of responsibility are often in conflict. The authorities, for example, burden us with a responsibility to obey them by means of numerous laws and threats of punishment, but we want to be free to decide how we want to live."

"A simple question of order or anarchy."

"Or we feel a responsibility to be kind to our dear ones, but at the same time to be absolutely sincere with them. But being kind to them doesn't always agree with being sincere."

"I understand you less and less."

"I mean to say that the world of responsibilities is a mine field in which even the smallest mistake can cause an explosion of unanticipated consequences."

"Then how are we supposed to live?"

"Like me."

"Rejecting all responsibilities and living exactly according to our inclinations, desires, and impulses?"

"Why not?"

"As soon as we decide on life without responsibilities, we've decided on a responsibility that is more fatal than all others combined."

"What then? Should we fall in love with responsibility?"

"You're close to the heart of the answer. What is the opposite of responsibility to another but love?"

"Are you joking?"

"Contrary to responsibility, which means *I must, I'm forced to, I have no choice, it's expected, it's proper*, and so on, love means *I desire, I want to, I'm attracted to, I yield to, I'm uplifted, I like*, and so on."

"Do you mean that we can substitute the feeling of responsibility with love for responsibility?"

"Not for responsibility. Love for things that life is made of."

"That's impossible."

"After all, it's nothing more than changing your point of view."

"One of the most widespread illusions."

"Do you know the story of the Zen Buddhist monk who came to a mountain monastery to achieve enlightenment?"

"I heard it but don't remember the details."

"The head, the master, gave him a responsibility. Every day he had to bring two buckets of water from the spring in the valley up to the mountain monastery. He did this for ten years."

"And for ten years he asked himself why his path to enlightenment was made up of nothing more than carrying out the monotonous duty to bring water to the monastery."

"I knew you were familiar with the story."

"Go on."

"After ten years, one day, tired and worn out on the mountainside, it seemed to him that no one's life is anything other than carrying out monotonous responsibilities. He realized that escape is always only escape to another responsibility. He had a feeling that he didn't have to go anywhere. That he didn't have to wait for or expect anything, because he already had his responsibility."

"And?"

"Isn't it marvelous? he said to himself. I carry water. The world is as it should be. He fell in love with his responsibility and set himself free."

"But is that really possible?"

"What?"

"Is it possible to fall in love with all the big and small irritations that make up the array of responsibilities in our everyday lives? To say to ourselves, isn't it marvelous to wait in the rain without an umbrella for a bus that's nowhere to be seen? Isn't it marvelous that the greater our efforts for people to understand and love us, the more they reject us?"

"Our chief responsibility is, of course, to be happy. But how are we to be happy if we're not capable of falling in love with what can't be avoided?"

"And if we are?"

"You think we are?"

"And that's our only solution?"

"I'm afraid that's no longer a solution for me."

"You inherited so much money from someone, maybe a rich uncle, that you can travel from place to place for the rest of your life without having ever to ask why you're doing it."

"How did you guess?"

"There's no other way."

"It's true that the inheritance changed my life plans quite a bit. Because of it, I can spend every other night on the opposite end of the world until the end of my life."

"And every other day get on another plane. Flying to

where? Nowhere. Away from responsibility? Your responsibility is to remain without a goal."

"That's not a responsibility."

"And what did you do before?"

"Before when?"

"Before your uncle left you a fortune."

"What boys my age usually do. I chased girls. And women your age. At the same time I tried, not very successfully, to study psychology."

"Too bad you didn't. Psychology would have been a big help to you."

"Does it seem to you that I'm ill?"

"What do you mean?"

"Ill because I don't want to stay in one place, in one job? Convinced that I've reached my goal? Not in the company of three friends until the end of life, but to be somewhere else every other day?"

"Never in my life have I met anyone even remotely like you."

"Is that criticism or praise?"

"Marvel."

"Thanks. And I've been sitting here for hours marveling at your breasts. Are they real or artificial?"

"Would you like to squeeze them? Then you'll know for sure."

"I would."

"But not here."

"I have a reservation at a comfortable hotel in Sydney, with a view of the bridge, the opera, and the bay."

"I can't promise. All I can say that the thought doesn't repel me."

"Although I have to warn you that you'll be just one of many."

"That goes for you, too."

***

"Where did we leave off?"

"My breasts, which you'd like to squeeze."

"Oh, yes. What if that weren't enough for me and I would want something more?"

"I'm ready to bargain."

"About money?"

"That, too. I expect at least two ice creams and a visit to the opera."

"I can arrange that."

"How long to you plan to stay in Sydney?"

"Maybe two days. Maybe three."

"I see you're counting on a long lasting love affair."

"We can exchange e-mails and meet every now and then at this or that end of the world."

"Will you reimburse my travel expenses?"

"Gladly."

"Depending on how much you like my breasts."

"And everything else that comes with them."

"In short, I'll have to prove myself."

"That goes for both."

"When did this travel bug infect you?"

"Several years ago. When I inherited the money. Soon after some strange emptiness emerged inside me, a tension before a storm, a pressure in my chest, all at once."

"Happiness went over the pass and became unhappiness."

"I would often look out the window into the distance and ask myself what to do now, when I didn't have to do anything? What good to anyone or anything was everything I suddenly had? I should get something from it, some fun or at least satisfaction."

"No doubt."

"But I only had strange, dark thoughts. As if a deadly disease were gnawing at me. Have you had feelings like that?"

"More than you think."

"They drove me to travel. From place to place, country to country."

"And? Did the pain disappear?"

"The pain is tolerable as long as I'm on the road or at home getting ready to leave."

"That means that sometimes you are at home."

"It's very complicated. I don't know if you'll understand."

"Women with large breasts also have brains. It's not the rule, but it happens."

"There are really two separate persons living in me. The first wants to keep going and moving. It exposes itself to adventures and dangers. The other would as soon stay between four walls and wait for the world to come and knock on the door."

"And when the world actually does knock on the door, that person would rather turn out the lights and pretend he's not home."

"How do you know?"

"That person is happiest when it's just fantasizing about the world. The other one, that can't find peace, is an adventurer. He doesn't want to stay on the sidelines, he wants to be part of the game. He wants to be the game."

"You know a lot about me."

"Doesn't it seem to you that these two people in you have a suspiciously good relationship?"

"What do you mean?"

"The one that prefers to dream about the world constructs a marvelous picture of new places in his imagination, and then waits for the other one to set off and check the picture."

"That's right."

"The report the second one brings back is negative: the world isn't like the first one imagined. The dreamer is more than pleased with the news, because it gives him the right to dream on."

"And the adventurer can barely wait to go and check the next picture of the world, constructed by imagination."

"And so they're both satisfied."

"Although there's a problem. They both live in one body. Which means that the first can't stay home when the other goes traveling."

"Exactly. And so the one who prefers to remain between four walls also has to wander through jungles, climb over passes, sleep with cockroaches and rats, work his way in a sweat through crowds, eat awful food, and avoid robbers."

"I think I've read this somewhere."

"We obviously read the same books."

"Have you ever been robbed?" asks the busty lady.

"Seven times."

"But they didn't kill you."

"Seeing that I'm here, probably not."

"Now that you're rich, you can certainly avoid the cockroaches."

"The most cockroaches live in the kitchens of the most expensive hotels."

"Even in the one in Sydney, where you want to squeeze my breasts, among other things?"

"We'll try to avoid the kitchen."

"Which won't be hard if we spend most of our time in bed."

"That's no longer a promise," says the dour young man. "That's a guarantee."

"I only decide so quickly above the clouds. The plane roaring through the air at such a speed obviously has an influence on me."

"As long as you don't change your mind later, when the plane lands."

"Would you be disappointed?"

"The adventurer in me for sure."

"Tell me something. Are you afraid of the moment when the traveler in you says that's enough, I'd rather take it easy?"

"I understand the question this way. Is it really smarter to stay at home, despite all the world seems to offer? Am I making a mistake devoting such a part of my life to aimless wandering? Is that what you're asking me?"

"How did you guess?"

"Doesn't it seem to you that travel is the best cure for boredom? For the depression caused by living under the same roof, repeating the same movements, sleeping in the same bed?"

"But your reason for constantly being on the road always to somewhere else is different, or at least you said so."

"We keep thinking up reasons for what we do, depending on the circumstances."

"Maybe I do the same thing but haven't noticed."

"When I don't go anywhere for a long time, my face grows longer, my eyes glaze over, and I get older. I become irritating, obnoxious."

"That's familiar."

"When I return from a long trip, I'm unbelievably rested and pleasant with even the biggest jerks, my eyes shine, and every day is a holiday."

"Right now it would be hard to say that your eyes are shining, because you're probably just at the beginning of your latest journey."

"Lately my eyes don't shine any more, not even after months of travel."

"But tell me, isn't it the same nowadays at all ends of the earth? Aren't all the planes alike, all the towns, all the supermarkets, all the skyscrapers, all the taxis, all the stores that sell the same things everywhere?"

"That's why I have a constant urge to go on."

"But the realization that only one body is sitting in the plane, although there are really two persons in it, surely doesn't give your relief."

"None at all."

"I'd say that it even deepens the torture of the fragmented subject traveling the world to find some glue to put the pieces of himself into a dish into which to pour the liquid of his being."

"Would you be offended if I were to ask you what you do?"

"Haven't you realized that I like offensive and unusual young men?"

"That's not an answer."

"The answer to your question will not only surprise you, but devastate you."

"I'm used to the worst."

"There are things that go beyond even cockroaches, lice, malaria, typhoid fever, dengue fever, river blindness, and everything else that plagues a person who is always on the road with only one goal—to discover why he's always on the road."

"Maybe you're right."

"Not because I'm older than you, but because your case is so transparent that even a child of average intelligence would recognize it. Much less a professor of philosophy at the University of London."

"That's what you are?"

"I was. Then something happened and fate directed my life elsewhere."

"You were seized by the urge to see the world before it was too late."

"No, I was seized by the urge to give the world as good as I got."

"I don't understand."

"I came into the world with potent curiosity. And with a need to seduce handsome young men. Well, men up to the age of fifty. Who are still fresh and young, now that life expectancy has increased."

"I see nothing wrong with that."

"I'm certainly not the only woman like that in the world."

"Everyone has a right to realize their essence."

"I wasn't a nymphomaniac, far from it. But I was about as interested in sex as in the unsolvable problems of philosophy. Not sex for its own sake, don't get me wrong, but the variations, all the male varieties."

"For the most part males are depressingly alike."

"I wanted to try different races, ethnicities, and degrees of intelligence. From trash collectors to geniuses. Although I have to say that I liked trash collectors best and geniuses least."

"A risky business."

"I figured that out too late. I caught HIV somewhere and now I'm a candidate for AIDS. That's why I changed from traveling from man to man to traveling from place to place."

"The question is to what end."

"To infect as many men as possible with the disease that in the end will kill me."

"Does that seem honorable to you?"

"It's unjust to reproach a woman who is dying at forty that she's dishonorable."

"I would find it hard to agree."

"Wasn't I honorable when I warned you what awaits you if you go to bed with me? In that beautiful Sydney hotel with a view of the harbor bridge and the opera."

"And why did you tell the truth to me?"

"Because I like you. Because you're just as sick, maybe even sicker than I am."

"I don't understand."

"I'm going to die because of lack of caution. You're going to live on, running from responsibilities, like a prisoner of the responsibility with which money enslaved you. I'll be saved by eternal silence, while you'll be tortured by your delusion for another half century. That's freedom to be thankful for."

"But you really don't mean that?"

"In fact I mean exactly that."

"I wouldn't give up hope. Nowadays there are medicines…"

"In the end nothing helps. The awareness of being HIV-positive informs your life, thinking, worldview, feelings, everything."

"What can I say…?"

"The only honorable answer is silence."

"Maybe that's right."

"Promise me just one thing. That despite what you know about me, I can spend at least one night with you in that hotel in Sydney."

"I don't know…"

"No sex. Just a close, let's say friendly embrace. And that in spite of everything you'll massage my breasts for a few hours. That's not infectious."

"True."

"For pleasure, not out of sympathy. Because I need it. For someone to massage my breasts with pleasure even though I'm sick."

"I'll try. If you promise me something."

"That is?"

"That you'll stop traveling the world out of a desire to infect as many men as possible. That's not you. That's just a reaction, not at all thought through, and at odds with you character."

"A traveler who's running from responsibilities has started moralizing?"

"I promise you can spend several nights with me. I promise we'll go to the opera. Maybe *Tristan and Isolde* is on. In turn, you promise me you'll stop behaving contrary to what you are."

"What am I?"

"An unhappy person that fate has led astray, like me, and turned from the light to darkness."

"All I can say is that I'll do all in my power to fulfill your wish."

"In the given situation, that's enough."

"You promise me something?"

"What??

"From this moment on not one sound, much less a word about my disease."

"What would it mean to anyone?"

"True. I have to get used to being no one."

"That's the hardest thing. I've been trying for years."

5.

The Devil's Work

"You're kind of pensive. What's eating you?"

"Maybe we're not the best parents for the child we plan on adopting."

"Why not?"

"Because you believe in God, and I believe in the Devil."

"Oh, come on. Since when do you believe in the Devil?"

"I put that wrong. I'm afraid that the Devil created the world, not God."

"What's the matter with you?"

"God is supposed to be almighty and good. And the Devil is a fallen angel who is only supposed to vex Him."

"And that's what he's doing."

"You don't understand. Look…"

"Didn't Pascal already state that God is not almighty, because he can't build a wall that he couldn't jump over?"

"That's just a logical paradox…"

"Everything connected with God is a logical paradox. The same with the Devil."

"Let's start at the beginning."

"The Big Bang?"

"Look, I'd like a serious conversation about serious things."

"Go on."

"Already in the nineteenth century, John Stuart Mill ridiculed God, not only as a creator, but also his characteristics."

"Philosophers are known for striking out blindly."

"Look at the world, look at history."

"It's not a pretty picture."

"Billions of people suffered, suffer, and will continue to suffer from disease, hunger, wars, and terrible deaths."

"Yes, and?"

"Billions of people suffer because they can't help people who are suffering even worse than those who are suffering intolerably."

"That's not quite true."

"You know quite well that the money intended for those who are suffering almost never reaches them."

"I think you had something else in mind."

"I wanted to say that God created the world, if he really did, without the slightest trace of what is called empathy. What happens when the people dearest to us die? We suffer. And when we suffer, so do those dearest to us. Children slave in factories, women slave for pimps, extremists behead their victims and display the pictures on social media."

"Someone should intervene."

"Who? America?"

"Someone who is really almighty. God."

"He's clearly on the sidelines."

"Why? Because He's malevolent or because He's not almighty?"

"Maybe there's something equally at odds with logic: partial almightiness. Maybe there're no absolutes."

"Do you ever think about animals?"

"You mean our cat, that are neighbor is taking care of in London?"

"Do you ever think about how billions of animals in the world suffer? And I don't mean cows, sheep, goats, and others that we raise in cages that they can't turn around in before we cruelly slaughter and eat them."

"Have a drink. Because what you've started on…"

"Billions of animals without freedom, suffering unbearable pain, are killed and eaten by other animals whose turn then comes to be agonizingly killed and eaten. Do you ever think about that?"

"Does anyone think about that?"

"How does the Devil feel when he hears people in millions of churches, mosques, and temples singing God's praises?

"I don't know. Ignored?"

"And who wouldn't? When it's quite clear the prize went to the wrong, more likeable candidate."

"As often happens."

"So then, who created the world, God or the Devil?"

"Does it matter?"

"Maybe. But why did God or the Devil create a world so permeated with evil?"

"I see that you want argue."

"Yes, I want to argue."

"If God created the world, all the torments people suffer are a result of God in his wisdom having given people free will. Would you want to live in a world where you couldn't choose?"

"I don't know."

"But the Devil would have created people with free will, too. After all, he would have known that most would opt for deceit, lies, misdeeds, injustice, and evil. And he would have had only one opponent—a pretty unsuccessful one—in God."

"Look…"

"Doesn't the Devil rub his hands when he sees all this? Isn't he angry when he sees that people don't credit him with what's going on, but nature, which is not supposedly isn't connected with God, although, as believers say, God created it?"

"But there're also a lot of fun and happy moments in

the world."

"That's true."

"If the Devil created the world, why would he also create things that God would have created?"

"Because such things don't last long and they result in disappointment, sadness, and despair. A guilty feeling, jealousy, anxiety—none of which God would ever create."

"But those are all human feelings that depend on chance, decisions, and actions."

"You forgot about something. The Devil left billions of people uncertain as to whether God even exists. Isn't that the worst torment he foisted on people?"

"Excuse me, but I don't understand certain things that we're discussing so eloquently but quite senselessly."

"Which ones?"

"If God really exists and if He did create the world, why should He be boundlessly good? Were it not for evil existing as well, we would have no idea of the good. Isn't it the contrast that allows us to recognize the difference between the two?"

"I think an elderly Devil created the world as a senile joke, and God is trying to fix it like an innocent child."

"Can I remind you of something?"

"Go ahead."

"Of my sister, who was going home from work in London, on a bus. She was with her boyfriend, and they were deciding whether to rent an apartment they had looked at the day before. A normal, everyday conversation, don't you think?"

"Go on."

"At one of the stops a young man gets on, just as normal, but with one exception: he was wearing an overcoat in the middle of summer."

"There are plenty of oddballs."

"Under the overcoat he was hiding a bomb, sharp nails, round pellets, and rat poison."

"I think I know what you're going to say."

"Nonetheless, he gave the other riders a friendly smile."

"Well, that's what the witnesses said."

"And then, at one of the next stops, he pressed the button on the bomb. It blew him away, along with my sister and her fiancé, twenty other people, including children, and half the bus."

"We live in terrible times."

"An everyday occurrence?"

"Unfortunately."

"But something isn't everyday. That the parents of the suicide bomber that killed so many innocent people voiced pride in his success. In their opinion, he went straight to heaven and can prepare a suitable place for them as well. Friends and relatives brought them gifts and expressed their admiration."

"The Devil's work."

"No doubt about it, but tell me something. Why don't we know anything about that boy's personality, how he got along with kids at school. Was he generous, modest, social? We know nothing about this. But we can easily guess his religion."

"Muslim."

"But surely there were other important things in his life. Was he in love? Was he a racist? Did he have friends? Did he confide in them? Did they confide in him? We don't know any of this. Only that he was Muslim. And we found out as soon as news of the attack became public."

"What does that have to do with God?"

"I'm talking about religion."

"Religion is unrelated to God."

"I want to say that everything in your life—your thoughts, feelings, actions—determine what you believe in."

"I know that…"

"Why are we flying to Australia? Because we

decided to adopt a child. A four-year old little boy who is going to have two fathers instead of a mom and dad."

"Which he still doesn't know."

"But he'll find out. And then?"

"We'll see."

"We decided to adopt this wonderful little boy, an orphan, because now the law permits it. And because we believe that a gay couple can provide a child security and a normal upbringing just as well as a heterosexual one."

"No doubt about it."

"What, then, is the basis for our actions? Faith."

"Why else would we be sitting on this plane?"

"To return to faith in God, to religion. Most people in the world believe that God created it and at the same time wrote a list of rules for how to live in it."

"The Bible."

"But the problem is we have many such books, written by different gods. And each one claims the title of the only true one."

"Again, the Devil's work."

"And people form groups according to which of these divine books they regard as most true."

"My God against yours. Sacred scriptures oblige us to believe and to do some good things, and everything that's good is common to all. But in each of them there is incitement to actions that the Devil thought up."

"Perhaps God really did write a holy text, each his own, because they're so different, but the Devil was the editor who struck out certain parts and replaced them with his own."

"For example."

"Let's take the possibility that our son, when he's eighteen, will come home from yoga exercises and tell us we have to follow the teachings of the god Krishna. What will we do?"

"By then I'll be too stiff for yoga."

"Do you know what kind of punishment the gods intended for people like us?"

"You mean fags?"

"If you insist on using that word."

"An eternity of hell fire."

"I'm not talking about the gods but about sacred texts."

"Nowadays they ought to be classified as hate speech."

"How are we going to raise our child?"

"I don't know."

"We won't be able to avoid the question of God. And if we're honest, you and I aren't atheists either."

"We'll have to think up something new."

"A new religion? A new god?"

"Why not?"

"Don't be ridiculous. We'll be living in Christian surroundings. Parish schools are the best. Sooner or later the child will be contaminated. And then what?"

"We'll contaminate him before other's have a chance. We'll teach him that he can discover God and really get close to Him only through physics and cosmology."

"Are you joking?"

"You don't agree with me?"

"After all, we can't each have our own God."

"Of course not. And why not? Because the only path to God is through knowledge."

"Let's forget God once and for all and talk about how we'll raise the child. I have to say that I'm afraid."

"Why?"

"It won't be simple."

"What in this world is?"

"To a certain extent I've reconciled myself to having to play the role of mom."

"The food cart is here. What'll you have? We'll continue on a full stomach."

"I hope we won't start arguing now already about how we are going to…"

"We don't even have the child yet. We're on the way to get him. Maybe he'll hate us as soon as he sees us. Maybe he'll throw himself on the floor and say he's not going anywhere."

"I have a good feeling."

The stewardess leans over. "Chicken or fish?"

***

"You should be happy but you're more and more worried."

"Do you have any idea what a four-year old child eats?"

"That can't be a mystery. All the children on the plane got a special child's meal."

"Are you counting on one of the flight attendants living with us?"

"Children eat the same things as adults, only in smaller portions."

"Are you sure?"

"Besides, a four-year old can choose what he wants to eat."

"And if he would want things that could harm his health"

"You know what? Your worries are a little irritating. It seems to me you don't actually want the child. You're already seeing him as a burden."

"Isn't it normal to worry? Like all parents?"

"There will be problems, be we'll solve them as we go."

"And what will we do if he hates us?"

"Are you afraid of that?"

"Children hate their parents. Even normal parents."

"Then you admit that as fags we won't be normal

parents."

"We agreed not to use that word. And never in front of the child."

"But sooner or later—I'd say very soon—the child will confront the fact that his parents are different."

"That's just why. The Devil, who created the world and the church, will sooner or later—very soon, as you said—open his eyes, and he'll see that fate played a trick on him and he'll never have a mom in his life."

"But he doesn't have one now."

"And if a time comes when he wants one, so he has one like most of the kids at school? If he gets tired of being different?"

"We'll deal with that when it happens. If it does."

"You think it won't?"

"That depends on how we raise him."

"Well, tell me. How?"

"I admit it will be a problem, but an aboriginal Australian child among white Europeans would have problems even if his family were normal."

"Again you're saying that we're not normal."

"I don't mean that. If others considered it normal."

"But in our case that won't happen. The child will come home from school crying and pretty soon he'll hate us. You can count on the Devil seeing to that."

"Kindly leave the Devil out of it."

"The Devil can hardly wait for a chance to destroy love where it could be most sincere."

"Our child will be happiest if he never hears the words God and Devil."

"Then he shouldn't read the Bible?"

"We'll always be absolutely honest with him. We'll introduce him to everything that's wrong with the world and with people, and why they don't all think alike, but we'll leave decisions to him. After all, he has a certain genetic code, which we know nothing about."

"He might even be a murderer because of his genetic code, and he'll kill his abnormal parents when he is twenty."

"Some will say he did a good deed."

"You know what I'm most afraid of? That he'll reject us the first time we meet. You shouldn't explain your feelings to children."

"What if it's the opposite? And we don't see in *him* what we desire?"

"I can't imagine that."

"I can."

"Do we have any idea what we want?"

"A beautiful, smart child who is going to fill our relatively empty lives and change us into better persons."

"We also have to give one of the Devil's victims comfort, and education, and beautiful future."

"We can try, but it's impossible to predict the results."

"I'm actually getting ever more frightened."

"If you believed in God, He would comfort you now, filling you with courage. But the Devil is ever more insistently whispering to you that you're right."

"But you don't believe in God."

"That's my personal matter. The problem is that you believe in the Devil."

"I didn't say I believe in him, I only said that God couldn't have created the world. Such as it is, it could only have been created by the Devil. Who is the real ruler of the universe and our hearts."

"And that's what we'll tell the child?"

"Why not tell him the truth right at the start?"

"Then you know very little about raising children."

"I'm ready to learn from you, Great Master."

"I have nothing to tell you. Because I don't know anything. But even though I don't, I have no worries. We'll raise the child as we go. Step by step he'll show us the way."

"But we do need some general plan."

"I don't know. What is the Devil whispering to you about this?"

"In the best case, the Devil will cancel all of our plans, and when that happens, don't dare say to me that it was God who did it."

"You know what, we can't talk about raising a child this way, in a spirit of superstition and naivety."

"Superstition?"

"For God's sake, every once in while we can enjoy a stupid debate about who created the world and why, but let it be our private fun. Let's not let it intrude on the life we live. That all three of us will have to live if we get the child."

"Everything's signed, all the papers are in order."

"We still have an interview. The social services office can still decide that we're not suitable parents, and the child can still say he doesn't want to go with us. There's still a chance that we'll return to London without him."

"And what can we do to prevent that?"

"Keep God and the Devil out of the game. If you're not ready to do that, I withdraw from the adoption."

"Why?"

"Because the child will grow up in an unhealthy environment."

"And what would *you* do, how would *you* raise him?"

"First of all I'd like to cultivate his courage not to pay too much attention to what others think of him, but find his true value in himself."

"I don't object to that."

"I'd like to convince him not to do things he doesn't want to, because he'll suffer as a result."

"And for absolutely nothing."

"I'd like to instill in him an awareness of how important it is to know what he wants in life and what he expects. And I'd like him to know that as soon as possible."

"In two, three years, perhaps?"

"I want to teach him that he must not be afraid to say

what he thinks. And not to associate with people he does not care for. And not to avoid people only because he's afraid of them."

"That won't be easy."

"The hardest thing for him will be not to copy others. To make his own decisions."

"If he has good parents, that won't be hard for him."

"But most of all I'd like to explain to him how wrong it is to think that people don't care for us. Because in most cases they're indifferent. In most cases they're not even aware we exist."

"Are you aware that I exist?"

After a short silence. "I'm afraid I'm not. On this plane, an hour or two ago, it suddenly occurred to me that I'm sitting next to someone who is not at all who I thought he was."

"Wait a minute…"

"My desire to adopt a child was pure. It filled me with courage and presented me with dreams I didn't know I had."

"The same with me."

"Then less than half an hour ago a thought crept into my head that I'm mistaken. That I'm mistaken about you *and* me. That I'm mistaken about us."

"Wait a minute…"

"Aren't we just two homosexuals who like each other physically, while mental differences between us remain unbridgeable?"

"Look, the part about the Devil was just…"

"I know. Blabbering. Like most of what you're able to put out. But that's not enough for me. I'd like to have a partner who might be less physically attractive than you but who possessed a little more common sense. Not wisdom, that's always a rarity. Just common sense."

"And I possess too little."

"Don't take it personally. Although there's no other

way to take it. But our plan to adopt a child and raise him as a family is in the end an illusion. Don't you think?"

"Then why are we going to Australia?"

"I doubt we'll get the child after they test our relationship and each of us individually. And if we do, we'll never come together on raising it. Even now you're worried about what he'll eat. He'll eat food, what else. Food that he likes. Even now you think more of yourself than of the child."

"That's not true."

"Let's put it this way. I'm the one who doesn't want to adopt the child. I changed my mind. I'm convinced the child will be unhappy with us."

"What about the money we paid the agent to arrange the adoption?"

"We'll forget about it. In any case, *I* paid it. I made a mistake. Two."

"And I'm the other one."

"Maybe."

"And what must I do?"

"Stop believing that the Devil created the world. We don't know how the world came to be, but it exists. The result of a chain of coincidences. Just like everything else. Like our meeting and relationship. Things happen and then come apart. Stop believing that the child will save our bond."

"Are you trying to say that our bond is broken?"

"I don't know. Maybe. Maybe not."

"And what does it depend on?"

"On you."

"What must I do?"

"The outcome doesn't depend on what you do or don't do, but on which way my feelings go. I don't have control of that."

"And when will I know?"

"Not before me."

"Are you aware of how cruel you are?"

"Only honest, my dear. Uncompromisingly honest. As I always was. While you were hardly at all."

"Not only the world, but you, too, are the Devil's creation."

"And a blind one. Otherwise we wouldn't be on this plane."

6.

Shades of Sorrow

"A long flight, isn't it?" sighs a young lady with glasses sitting by the window, turning slightly to her middle-aged neighbor who is vacantly staring ahead.

"I'd say so," replies the gentleman in elegant dark gray and a black tie.

"Were you at a funeral, or are you going to one?"

"Because of the tie? No, no, I have only three and they're all black. My wife bought me all three."

"She obviously likes black."

"Her clothes are black, too. Even the sheets and towels in our home are black."

"Does that bother you?"

"Not at all. I'm a funeral home director. And my wife works there as my assistant."

"Interesting," the young woman with glasses says politely and not quite convincingly. "In London or Australia?"

"In Sydney. I hope you're not bothered by sitting next to a funeral home director."

"Should I be?"

"Only if you're superstitious. It's true, though, that my wife and I don't have many friends. In fact, we're pretty lonely. As if we were to blame for people dying."

"That's absurd."

"As most things in this world."

"I agree. I'm returning from my aunt's funeral in Liverpool. And with whom do I have the pleasure?"

"That's a coincidence. I'm returning from a school reunion in Slovenia. Thirty-five years."

"In Slovenia? That's another coincidence. My best friend is from Slovenia. She and I studied together in Melbourne. Law. We're both lawyers."

"Interesting."

"How was the reunion?"

"I'd almost rather not talk about it."

"I felt you're kind of depressed."

"Is it that obvious?"

"Unless it's related to your occupation."

"No. I'm really pretty upbeat by nature."

"Then it's the reunion."

"Of course, you're too young…"

"Oh, not that young that I wouldn't attend reunions. And every time I return strangely down, too."

"Maybe I'm too much of an idealist."

"Are you really a funeral home director?"

"I write songs in my free time. For clients. Mourning songs that my wife then sings at funerals as part of the ritual. My wife has a very beautiful voice."

"It did seem to me there was something soft inside you."

"A reunion should also be a ritual. A serious thing. Hallowed."

"Wasn't it?"

"It was mostly an occasion for a good dinner, drinking, and jealous checking on who had aged more."

"And who had achieved more."

"Of course, we all avoided direct questions and tried to find out about occupations and work in a roundabout way. As if we weren't interested. Most of all we looked at cars. I had a rental, the least expensive."

"Did you tell your classmates where you work?"

"That would have poisoned the atmosphere even more."

"Probably true."

"As it was there was a feeling of painful nostalgia, almost gave me the shivers."

"Maybe only you."

"Everyone."

"Are you sure?"

"Perhaps we shouldn't have visited the classroom where we sat for four years before going to dinner. The past thirty-five years hovered over us like a kind of blunder, a bad dream between chemistry and math. It was as if we were students on break who went down the hall and returned to the classroom as ladies and gentleman fixed in the occupations and lives fated to us."

"But the mood must have improved at the restaurant."

"Not in the least. Despite the good food and even better wine, the topic of conversation didn't rise above exchanging information about missing classmates and opinions on domestic and international current events."

"That's painful."

"It wasn't painful, but it wasn't especially pleasant either."

"I know, I've experienced that, at a ten-year reunion."

"The most unusual thing seemed to me that we remained distant, fixed in relationships from our school years. As if we really hadn't grown up. As if we didn't have thirty-five years of life behind us."

"I know. A desire to chat and get close, along with the hope the whole thing won't last too long."

"The conclusion that we're still the same as we were, and at the same time politeness fitting for conversations with passing acquaintances."

"Exactly it. And every one of you was mumbling to himself in his own way about the cruel indifference of passing time."

"You know a lot about these things."

"And the numbing disappointment of life passing without rewarding anyone with what he wished for at graduation."

"It's unlikely you felt like that at your ten-year reunion."

"Time is relative."

"And the next day everyone was forced in his own way to ponder the sense of continuing in the given condition formed by a mix of personal choices and coincidences."

"Everyone felt in his own way a need to return to the past and take inventory."

"That's odd."

"What?"

"That reunions are so similar. Regardless of how much time has passed."

"Actually mine wasn't quite that way. I read about your feelings in some book—I don't recall the title—in which the author describes his feelings after a thirty-five year reunion using almost your exact words."

"Do you remember the author's name?"

"Unfortunately not."

"Then your ten-year reunion wasn't like that."

"It really wasn't that different, only the feelings were less intense. Still relatively young we believed that everything that hadn't come true was still ahead of us. Besides, we women experience things differently."

"How's that?"

"For a man, the realization that he scored only one goal, not ten, is very depressing."

"Because we're more ambitious?"

"Aren't you?"

"But you're a lawyer. What else do you want become?"

"And you're a business owner. Isn't that enough?"

"You probably *wanted* to become a lawyer, but I

never dreamed I would someday run a funeral home."

"What did you want to be?"

"After graduation I studied languages. English, German, and for some reason Dutch, too. I wanted to translate the classics."

"Did you finish your studies?"

"I was slow and unorganized, and I traveled a lot during that time. I didn't travel, I wandered. I met a young Australian woman on Bali and fell in love. She invited me home and introduced me to her parents. Her father was a funeral home director. Everyone wanted me to stay, we married, and not long after her parents died in a car accident. Someone had to take over the business."

"Who else but you."

"Actually my wife inherited it. She didn't want to sell, and begged me to take it over. She promised to help me."

"You had no reservations?"

"A good many at first. But our first child was on the way, I loved her, and it quickly became clear to me that I had no choice."

"That you were trapped."

"That fate had given me a less than ideal part, but I nevertheless had to play it. The thought of my family life passing among corpses frightened me, but I slowly grew inured to it."

"And now the corpses no longer bother you."

"I look at it all from a strange distance. My wife and I try to afford the dead a dignified burial. The clients are satisfied, and so are we. My wife convinced me that we're benefiting society."

"A successful marriage, a successful business. And you don't have to worry about a lack of customers."

"That sounds slightly cynical."

"Sorry. But then why, if everything in your life is so absolutely right, that great sadness on your face? And in your heart?"

"You can even see into my heart?"

"Through your eyes."

"Are you really a lawyer?"

"It's not important. Maybe I'm a fortuneteller. Or something like that. Just don't tell me that the sadness is a result of the reunion you're returning from."

"Why not?"

"It's too deep. There's no sign of it passing. You've been carrying it with you your whole life. As soon as you fastened your belt and gave me a quick glance, I said to myself, Mr. Sad is sitting next to me. And he's so handsome. You're probably aware of how handsome you are. I don't know if I've ever seen a more handsome man."

"Be so kind as to tell me where this is going."

"If a man sad that to a woman, both would know what he's fishing for. Women are different. If I wanted to seduce you, I'd go about it differently. And let's be honest: no man would turn around to look at me on the street."

"Don't exaggerate, you're very attractive."

"What spoils my looks are the bulging eyes behind the thick lenses of these angular glasses, my flat breasts, and the fat noticeably spilling over my belt."

"Looks are superficial, the soul matters."

"Exactly. And why has so much sadness settled on your soul?"

"I'm afraid you are shifting our conversation to a subject I don't feel really good about."

"You don't feel good about any subject. Why don't you admit it?"

"Those are personal matters."

"Why don't you entrust a complete stranger you'll never see again with everything that's weighing on you and you don't dare tell your wife?"

"Because I don't feel any special desire to do so."

"You don't trust me."

"That's not it. You've manipulated me into a position in which I have to defend myself, although I don't see a reason why I should do so."

"I'm manipulative?"

"I didn't say that. You probably are a lawyer, and a very good one. After all, you've been craftily interrogating me for quite a while. As if you were going to prove that I put live people into the ground."

"You do?"

"Oh, for God's sake..."

"I'd like to talk about your sadness. About its causes. Because I, too, am sad. Didn't you notice? You didn't, because you haven't even looked at me. Are you afraid?"

"Should I be?"

"You say you have to defend yourself, but in fact you're attacking me."

"What did I say that might be understood as an attack?"

"That I'm interrogating you."

"That's how I feel."

"Feelings are not enough for an indictment. And indictment without evidence is an attack."

"Can we stop?"

"Why now, just when it's gotten interesting?"

"Maybe for you, but not for me."

"For you, too, but you don't dare admit it."

"All this has gone too far."

"I'd like to talk about your sadness. And mine. Maybe we'll find points in common. And discover the reason for it."

"Oh, for God's sake..." The man gets up. "I'm going to the restroom."

***

"I'm surprised you dared to come back."

"I asked them to move me, but they said they overbooked the flight, so they won't, unless someone physically attacks me."

"Do you want me to do that?"

"Almost."

"That's how much you hate me?"

"You really don't get it that you're annoying me?"

"Do you want me to stop?"

"Please be so kind."

"Then I will. If you promise me something."

"What?"

"That you'll listen to me. I won't ask you anything. I'll do all the talking. About my sadness. And about how it seems to me that I know where it comes from. And how much it resembles yours."

"You can talk about your sadness. But leave my sadness, as you call it, alone, although it's really something different. If you say one word about it, I'll go and complain that you physically attacked me."

"You'll need a good lawyer. You can hire me, I'm not expensive."

The man sighs and leans back. "Right. Don't make it long. Otherwise I'll have to take three sleeping pills."

"What's to follow, Mr. Undertaker, conductor of souls to the next world, and author of mourning songs his wife sings at funerals, is the story of my sadness. Only my sadness, which is unlike the sadness of anyone else in the world. Except maybe of someone I promised not to mention it to."

"There you go."

"Can I continue?"

"Be my guest."

"There's a light inside me that shines too dimly yet wants to illuminate everything or at least some of that which the intellect can't apprehend and the heart yearns for."

"Continue."

"I'm looking for answers to questions that remain inside like the residue of a past disease, like a pain that can't be eased by wine, or company, or knowledge."

"Maybe with sex?"

"I'll ignore that. Some people don't even know that their experience of the world, even in the best instance, is not what it could be. Some live like a wound up clock, tick-tocking day in day out, without worry. They give themselves up to feelings shallow or deep, and thoughts intelligent or stupid without asking where they come from, how they arise, or where they lead. Some are satisfied with that."

"Aren't we all?"

"Among the many for whom internal anxiety seems a normal state, there are some who don't want to spend their lives in a den of ill-conceived and half uttered truths."

"But?"

"But want to break through to greater light, exchange their lanterns for the Sun."

"There are few such people."

"That's the way it seems, because a sea of mediocrity washes over us from all sides. So it seems that only isolated searchers who are too odd to pay them serious attention look for the Sun. Which is far from the truth. Their number is increasing. There are ever more people yearning to raise themselves from stupor into a waking state, from passivity to action."

"Are you sure?"

"In almost every person not condemned to darkness and ruin there lives a desire to pull down the walls of everyday life and move to a more open space. To put aside the burden of delusions and errors and to breathe freely."

"You speak as if you had memorized all this."

"I'm not talking about neurotics and psychotics, nervous and depressed individuals. I'm talking about people who are normal in most respects, responsible, more or less educated, and emotionally balanced. But who are nonetheless unhappy. Because sadness has settled over them."

"And you're one of those people."

"Just like you."

"You promised…"

"In short, the two of us. Maybe the only two on this plane, for Sadness with a capital letter chooses to nest only in exceptional individuals."

"Funeral home directors…"

"I'm talking about spiritual exceptionality, not secular success."

"Unhappy women who can't accept their physical appearance…"

"Well, we've made progress. You've admitted that I physically repulse you."

"I haven't given it a thought. By coincidence we've been seated together on a flight to Australia, struck up a conversation that I'm sorry I didn't avoid to start with, and you want to weave this into a story—God knows what kind and why—suitable for nothing more than a women's magazine, full of amateur philosophy not befitting a lawyer, if that's what in fact you are."

"You still don't see that I want to help you?"

"Me?"

"I'm inviting you on a journey together from sadness to happiness. The way is full of pitfalls, but I know them and can take you safely past them."

"If you know the pitfalls, you've already made the journey and ought to be happy. Yet you said you want to talk about sadness."

"The first journey is not necessarily successful. You have to make it many times. It's not simple to escape sadness once it's nested in your soul. That's why it's better for as many as possible to take the journey."

"Strength in numbers."

"I invite you to join the group I lead in Sydney. You

won't be sorry."

"Group? What are you? A therapist?"

"A savior to people broken by life who want to make a new one."

"And how did you decide I'm broken by life?"

"By the sadness in your eyes."

"And that's how you recruit people for your group? Strangers on planes? And probably even on trains and buses?"

"My rule is that I only invite people whose sadness is so great that it moves me."

"And mine has moved you?"

"Greatly. You're yearning for one thing, for freedom, but you don't dare escape, because you think it would be petrifying."

"Are you aware that our conversation is getting ever more bizarre?"

"Because you don't want to pay attention."

"I'm listening, but I don't know what and where is the part I'm not paying attention to."

"You might be listening, but you attribute meaning to my words that they don't have. The classic defense of a man when he doesn't want to be convinced of something."

"It can also be an inability to understand what you're actually talking about and what you do in that group of yours."

"You do know. But your cloak of sadness is so thick that you can't break through it to the depths below. To where truth lives in you."

The man sighs. "This is getting stressful."

"Not any more than burying dead people every day and keeping your senses while doing so."

"You're right. Why pretend? It really does demand an effort."

"You got up the courage to agree with me. We're making progress."

"What are people's occupations in your group?"

"Everything from grocer to high school principal. There're also a surgeon, tax inspector, bank teller, and whatever else."

"And what they have in common is that a great sadness."

"We've finally started a conversation."

"And what do you do in the group?"

"We search for answers to the fundamental questions that daily shove us into sadness's embrace. The answers are somewhere beyond the mountains we know as psychology, philosophy, science, and religion. Beyond the cliffs illuminated by the searchlights of rationalism that block our access to the unexplored plateaus beyond. Even though the answers to the questions that open our hearts to sadness are found precisely there, on those plateaus."

"And you lead this expedition."

"Someone has to."

"Well, at least you're not at a loss for verbal abilities."

"Don't forget I'm a lawyer. Was. Ever since I formed the group I stopped practicing law. Defending crooks and lying in the bargain is not for me. That's when my great sadness started."

"Why?"

"I was trapped, just like you."

"In law?"

"In unavoidable sociability. In endless parties in rich houses of rich clients, where the guests were almost always rich owners of other rich houses. And I was forced to listen to endlessly boring conversations of endlessly boring people—for that's how such rich people get, especially when there's a bunch of them—and into the bargain smile and pretend that totally uninteresting things greatly interest me. I myself built a nest for sadness, which like a big black chicken then started laying eggs in me. I simply couldn't find anyone in my professional circle that could be a friend to me. A real, true friend. I became terribly lonely. The way you and your wife are because of the work you do."

"Well, at least we have each other."

"I have the group. And we're all friends in the group."

"But why have you chosen as clients people who have taken you so far? The law encompasses all spheres of life. You could have defended the rights of immigrants, the homeless, and asylum seekers. You wouldn't bee lonely with them."

"I know. But when I realized my mistake it was too late."

"And you started the group."

"I didn't. First I joined it and searched for an answer. An older woman from Melbourne was leading it. She didn't want to tell us her occupation. But her sadness was smoldering for so long she couldn't overcome it. One day we found out that she threw herself from her apartment window on the twelfth floor. In her farewell note she expressed a desire that I take over the group and lead it on. At first I didn't want to, but then others expressed the same wish. In the end I didn't have a choice."

"Do you think the group would have broken up without you?"

"Probably. I was the most enthusiastic, the most dedicated. Perhaps because my sadness was the greatest and I, too, was in danger of ending like my predecessor. Perhaps I was at least a little selfish ad used the group with a goal in mind that seemed to be worth my life. That's what's saving me."

"How does the group work?"

"We meet in pairs, threes, small groups, and sometimes all together. I'm always present, it's regular work for me."

"And you talk and lecture. Are you also a teacher, an

instructor?"

"Far from it. We all work together. But it's true I lead the conversation, even intimate ones with individuals. I direct our search, make suggestions."

"And everyone trusts you."

"The group would break up without trust."

"That's for certain."

"Most of all they trust me because I sense I already know some paths through the mountains of established truths and at least twice in my life I've caught a glimpse of the plateau on the other side. And the group is growing. Whoever trusts me enough or is curious enough or is in such a bad situation that he would follow anyone anywhere quickly joins up with me. You will, too, I have no doubt."

"For the moment that seems impossible."

"Other moments will come."

"My work and family duties take up too much time."

"Which is the reason you'll join us sooner rather than later. And perhaps your wife?"

"My wife would make fun of all this."

"Some do. We're constantly subject to accusations, ridicule, and even hate. The ignorant say that we're involved with mysticism, black magic, that we're some kind of sect. Some insist there's nothing to search for, that it's an illusion, that everything is already clear. And that we should go and solve our problems with a psychiatrist. The most indulgent just smile."

"And you're convinced you'll find what you're looking for?"

"We're all aware that we might not reach the plateau beyond the mountains. The mass of established science is terrifying. And when we work our way through the thickets of opinions, theories, and proofs of all sorts of things, some among us are in fact tempted to stop and make a home in the embrace of a pleasant dogma or convenient hypothesis. It takes courage to think differently. Great courage. What keeps driving us on is the pain of sadness we bear inside. Sadness is unbearable pain. You don't feel the pain?"

The man sighs. "I don't really know."

"Of course, you do. It will be easier if you admit it."

"How many hours a week would I have to sacrifice if I joined the group?"

"As many as you want. It differs from week to week. Some are there every day, others less often, but most devote at least five hours a week to it."

"I don't know if I could manage."

"That's what everyone says. At the beginning. Then it sucks them in."

"And what do you live on now that you don't work as a lawyer?"

"Leading the group, how else."

"That means…"

"That means that every group member contributes ten percent of his monthly earnings to the group treasury. We use the money for operating expenses and renting the space where we meet. And my pay, of course."

"Then it's in your interest that more people join the group."

"Actually I expected you would come up with something like that. My pay varies. The group sets it every month by a majority vote. We use the remaining money to buy books, for bookkeeping, and for taxes. We're a registered organization."

"But you still strive to get as many new members as possible."

"We're guided by altruism. I often walk the streets of Sydney and look for people whose eyes shine with sadness. A special kind of sadness, something on the edge of despair. The sadness of a prisoner caught in a spider's web of the world's dogmas or responsibilities he took on in error. Such eyes shine with sadness and also fear."

"And then you invite them into the group."

"That's my responsibility."

"It seemed to me that that's how it works."

"How else could it?"

"I suspected there was money involved. Ten percent of monthly salaries is a lot. You can make a handsome sum that way. And if you're enterprising enough, it could turn out that you'll land up back at where you ran from. With an expensive house, among boring rich people who have nothing to talk about. A circular path from sadness back to sadness.

"How much does your company charge for a funeral?"

"Why?"

"Because I'm surprised you don't bury people for free and get by on the money you earn in some other job."

"Well… you're right about that."

"You know what? I don't want to talk with you anymore."

"Look, it's really too bad that…"

"If you're not quiet, I'm going to scream out loud that you're sexually assaulting me."

"You've just lost a potential group member."

"We don't need ones like you."

7.

Sex on Bali

"How unusual!" a beautiful young woman says to the man twenty years older sitting alongside.

"Unusual?" the man turns to her a main of brown hair that has started noticeably graying.

"Our meeting."

"Why?"

"I'm thinking of how fast we fell into each other's embrace."

"First into our eyes, and only then into an embrace."

"Into our eyes, heart, soul, and then embrace."

"And then into bed."

"And hardly two weeks later we're flying to Bali. Where three weeks of bliss await us."

"Or three days."

"Is that a threat?"

"It's up to you to explain my words. I don't want to deprive you of freedom."

"You know that I'll never cross you with what I say. So please choose your words carefully."

"Why?"

"It's possible I'll misunderstand something. And then I'll suffer instead of being happy."

"Does it seem right to you to shift the responsibility for your feelings onto me?"

"Is that what I'm doing?"

"You're dictating to me how to choose my words. You're making it impossible for me to express what I really feel."

"I'm constraining you?"

"I didn't say that. But I wouldn't want to feel that's what you're actually doing. Especially not on an island that you so want to see."

"Maybe I'm expecting too much. Our meeting sent me off the rails. I'm not thinking with my head but only with my heart."

"That's not bad. The heart is far more sensible than the head."

"Then you understand why I'm terrified when you say that they whole thing can end in three days?"

"And what if I was just expressing my own fear?"

"I didn't think of that."

"Well, think about me once in a while."

"But that's all I do. I'm thinking of you all the time!"

"You shouldn't."

"Why not?"

"Exaggerated excitement quickly becomes an obsession, and that inevitably ends in disappointment."

"You won't disappoint me."

"No?"

"I'll disappoint you first."

"First Bali will disappoint you, then I will."

"It's possible Bali will, but you, never."

"Are you sure?"

"Even if you leave me after two days, you'll always be the prince of my dreams."

"You didn't even know me before you came to my literary reading."

"Did you know me?"

"And you said it was your girlfriend who dragged you there. You said you hate poetry."

"That's what I thought. When I heard you read your poems, I suddenly realized that that's not really true, that poetry is something I miss most in my life."

111

"And from now on you'll read only poetry."
"For now, your poems are enough for me."
"But I really do hate poetry."
"How can a poet hate poetry?"
"Poets hate it most and most often. Readers are indifferent for the most part. You didn't hate it either; it just didn't interest you. That's no sin, because for a long time it has interested only a handful of people."
"And why do you hate it?"
"Because no poem is really good. Each one is a failed attempt."
"You can't be serious."
"I can try to explain, but I don't know if you'll understand."
"Because I'm not smart enough?"
"No, because I might not be smart enough to explain it so that you'd understand."
"Will you try anyway?"
"A true poet doesn't undertake to write a poem because he wants to represent himself to the public as a poet. He undertakes to write because he feels some transcendental impulse to connect with what lies behind all that is human, historical, and finite."
"To connect with the infinite?"
"I see you understand. As soon as the impulse turns into an actual poem, it's compromised by the finite word. You wish that the wheelbarrow would spread its wings and fly into the air, but then you see that it remains on the ground, because it's only a wheelbarrow. That's why every poem, even the best one, is a proof of failure."
"Am I to believe you?"
"There's a virtual poem, let's call it Poetry with a capital letter, there's abstract potential you feel when you undertake to write, but what comes about, the actual poem, is the complete opposite of what you intended to write, almost a sort of betrayal."

"But that doesn't go for everything?"

"Poems are the fatal problem of poetry. That's why poets most respect their peers who gather enough courage to stop writing."

"Some have done that?"

"Quite a few. The most famous is Rimbaud. He stopped writing poems when he was twenty and took up smuggling arms to Africa."

"At twenty?!"

"The best start early and quit early. But it's not at all the rule. Some labor their whole life and there are many good ones among them."

"But you're not thinking of quitting?"

"And if I were?"

"Don't you dare. Now that I'm in love with a poet, I want to have a poet. For a long, long time. All my life."

"Then you're not in love with me but with the poet in me."

"And what are you in love with?"

"A beautiful young, very sexy student of cultural anthropology, who because of my poems fell in love with something she was indifferent to before."

"I also have a soul. You just admitted that you're only in love with my body."

"I'll get to know your soul through your body."

"And if you decide I don't have one?"

"And if you decide that my poetry isn't what you're in love with, but you only like traveling the world with a famous poet?"

"Please, let's be serious. We'll have enough time for fun on the beach."

"You mustn't forget that most poems written throughout history have been bad. That means that among my poems there are many bad ones. Success and fame don't guarantee quality."

"You mean that everyone who praises you is

mistaken?"

"Not everyone, but most. If poetry is a chronicle of pathetic failures, then in my trade, the least successful are the ones who value poetry."

"And aren't, I assume, poets."

"Critics are a self-appointed caste of know-it-alls who any author worth his salt calmly ignores."

"You know that at first I wanted to study literature?"

"Good thing you didn't."

"In high school I dreamed about becoming a critic. So that I could critique others' works and prove I'm smarter and more capable than them."

"And?"

"I realized that I would first have to be capable of writing something better than what I was reviewing. I didn't want to lie, put on airs, and throw up some clichés. I'm too honest for that. Maybe it's a fault, but unfortunately that's how it is."

"If I find that's true, then my infatuation will probably turn into love."

"Is that possible?"

"Is it possible for your infatuation with a poet can change into love for an author of poems?"

"Don't you feel that has already happened?"

"Women are always in a hurry. We men are more cautious and keep testing our feelings. Women simply fall in love. And they quickly decide they made a mistake."

"Until now, I've missed having love in my life. You surely haven't."

"You missed love? You, with your beauty, who could give quite a few men a heart attack with one look?"

"I don't measure love by the number of men who would like to get me into bed."

"You're right. Now you see how stupid we poets are, especially the ones who at times dare think we're at least of average intelligence."

"You're exceptionally intelligent."

"That's experience. Don't forget that I'm twenty years older than you."

"Tell me about your experiences."

"Why would they interest you?"

"I want to know who you belonged to before you found yourself in my embrace."

"Let's talk about poetry."

"Which, as you said, we both hate."

"And justifiably, though for different reasons."

"I stopped hating it. Your poems awoke in me something I hadn't felt but was latently present in me all along."

"There's the possibility it won't last very long."

"You mean that after having stopped hating poetry you can hate it again?"

"You can hate the poet who made you love poetry."

"You are and always will be my poet. Mine and only mine, though I'm tormented by the fear that that's an illusion."

"It could be that the poetry dies before your love for me withers."

"I don't understand."

"Every so many years, culture critics enjoy pronouncing the death of poetry. They say that our imaginative capabilities have atrophied and that the commercialization of language has reached the extreme. Take a look at the more than three hundred thousand web pages devoted to poetry. Isn't that firm enough proof that poetry is dead?"

"Quite the opposite, I'd say."

"Are there three hundred thousand poets in the world? Poetry may have survived until now, but technology has finally killed it. If anyone can be a poet, the only honorable option for real poets is silence."

"But you're not silent."

"The poems you heard at the poetry reading where we met were written five years ago."

"And have you written any since then?"

"Not since then."

"You weren't inspired?"

"Inspiration is the empty nonsense of the ignorant. I haven't written anything for five years, because I hate the limits of every individual poem. Poetry with a capital letter surely exists, just as God with a capital letter must exist, but every individual, actual poem, once pronounced or written is but a parody, like the Bible, written and canonized, is a parody of the divine."

"Maybe poets expect poetry to achieve more than it can."

"To expect less would mean we're no longer searching for contact with the world, because we're satisfied with its shadow."

"You won't think me stupid if I say something?"

"That's hard, since we haven't agreed on a definition of 'stupid.'"

"Isn't it enough that some poems comfort or excite us, make us happy or entertain us, and that at rare moments they move and spark in us a desire for what is beautiful and sincere?"

"That's all very well and maybe sufficient for readers of poetry. Although it clearly isn't, given that there are ever fewer readers, almost fewer than writers of poetry. But it's in no way enough for true poets. Bad poets radicalize their failures and show in no uncertain terms that the path to connecting with true Poetry cannot be traversed. It's sad but true that you'll find the greatest mediocrity among award winning poets."

"At times I get the feeling that you're joking on account of my ignorance."

"Mostly I'm joking about my dependence on poetry, which I'd like to renounce. Most poems nowadays are bad, because the nature of time has distanced them form Poetry with a capital letter. And because they offer passing excitement only to rare individuals, without being able to actively penetrate society, and so they sound empty and die after the first reading. That's why I hate poems and continually yearn for Poetry."

"Who is to blame if that's how it is?"

"It's not the fault of poets, it's the fault of poems. Poetry in the soul of poets is boundless and absolutely full, but printed poems are more or less awkward facsimiles of what the poet wanted to convey to the reader. And through an ever smaller handful of readers to the world, which he would like to influence."

"I understand it this way: poems are to blame for their being bad, not their authors."

"If poems are more or less incomprehensible and inaccessible to all but a handful of super-intellectuals, they're elitist. If they're clichéd, they irritate us, because they show they're accessible to their audience only by virtue of a dead language, neutralized and impersonalized by its popularity. And if they're weapons in the hands of revolutionaries, which they often are, then they're fired like blanks."

"Then it's impossible to win?"

"Poets aren't liars because, as Socrates said, they can by blind us by the power of their imitations, but because by declaring yourself a poet you dedicate your life to overcoming the bitter logic of the poetic principle, knowing full well that that isn't possible."

"I'm afraid that I didn't quite understand a thing or two you said."

"I'm not surprised."

"Do you like me less for that?"

"Didn't we say that I like your body more than your brains?"

"Do you enjoy hurting me?"

"Do you enjoy not understanding my humor?"

"How am I to know when you're joking and when you're serious?"

"You can't, because you're not Aquarius but Virgo. Only Aquarians understand each other without having to say a word."

"Am I to blame for not being Aquarius?"

"Do you see now why Poetry is unachievable, and why I hate it?"

"At times I get the feeling that you're taking me to Bali because you'd like to do some experiment on me. And then write an essay about it."

"I don't write essays."

"Why don't you want to tell me about your past? Are you afraid I wouldn't like you afterwards?"

"Why don't you tell me about your past."

"What kind of past does a student have who just decided what she wants to study compared to the past of a poet at the peak of his fame?"

"Does our age difference bother you?"

"More you, it seems."

"Right. I'll tell you a few things about my past. If you tell me all about yours."

"My story will be short."

"That's alright. But first I'll go to the restroom."

* * *

"Well, my dear poet? You promised to tell me everything about your past."

"Not everything, I've forgotten most of it."

"Then tell me what you haven't."

"A few things will surprise you."

"For example?"

"For example that I like downpours, hedgehogs, and

fishing in a storm."

"Is the hedgehog your favorite animal?"

"I knew you wouldn't believe me."

"It seems unusual. Why exactly hedgehog?"

"Because despite its sharp quills, it's harmless. Lonely. It lives in constant fear. Because it's the only animal that cries."

"How do you know?"

"One day when I was on a walk, I heard a noise inside a hedge, and suddenly a hedgehog appeared before me on the small path. It was clearly in a good mood and on its way somewhere. I liked it so much that I picked it up and took it home to the cottage in the village where I lived at the time."

"Why did you do that?"

"I was lonely and wanted company."

"And it didn't resist?"

"It shot its quills, but I wrapped it in a rag and brought it safely home. I put it on the floor and offered it water, but it didn't touch it at all."

"Did you talk to it?"

"I discovered that we don't have a common language. And I got the feeling that it was even sadder about that than I."

"And then?"

"It wandered around the cottage as if it wanted to be intimately acquainted with every corner and every thing. I had to go to the bathroom, and when I returned, it was gone."

"Did it run away?"

"Whether it ran away or lost its way I'll never know. Although it seems to me more likely that it lost its way."

"And what did you do?"

"I went to look for it, what else. With a flashlight. It was night. Of course, it's hard to find a hedgehog at night, almost impossible."

"You didn't find it."

"A while later I heard an unusual sound, like a child crying, almost inaudible. I followed the sound to a heap of empty cardboard boxes. And what did I find? My prickly friend, letting out squeaking sounds of despair, his snout in a puddle of tears. It was really sobbing like a child who has been wronged."

"And what did you do?"

"In the rush of sympathy I wanted to kiss it. And I would have, had it not been covered with a blanket of quills."

"But why was it crying?"

"I don't know. Maybe it realized that we couldn't be friends."

"Why not?"

"Because we didn't have a language to exchange thoughts and share our feelings."

"And you?"

"Tears came to my eyes, too. I left him and went into the night. Aimlessly. Meantime, the weather got nasty and sheets of icy rain splashed over me, beating my face as if I were to blame that animals can't talk with us and suffer because of that. The wind toppled trees along the road, there was thunder and lightning as if it were Judgment Day. I really enjoyed it. Only extreme weather has the power to cleanse me of sadness."

"My dear…"

"The bad weather lasted until morning. When day dawned, the world was once again ordinary chaos—mud and downed trees all about, the sun in the foggy sky looked like a shriveled mushroom, the mud came up to my knees and it seemed to me that my heart was covered in it, too, as it took ceaseless effort to pump blood through me."

"And the hedgehog?"

"He was gone. He went his way. Maybe the downpour carried him into the nearby river."

"If you only knew how eternally in love I am with

you."

"Like a million people with a million others. It's an ordinary thing."

"Not for me."

"It will be when you wake from your dream."

"Tell me about fishing in a storm."

"It was only one time, five years ago, on Lake Victoria in Africa. My son and I were paddling into the night in small canoes against waves that were growing more powerful and deadly behind the wind of an approaching storm. We were average canoeists, and then above us exploded a bolt that literally looked like the fire of hell. There were oranges, blues, and greens in the flash. It was like arrows clashing into one another, and the thunder didn't stop. Then another little boat appeared close by, and we started competing with it. The waves splashed over both and the canoes were like ruffled feathers on giant birds, then like fish whose eyes burned as yellow as two traffic lights, burned from within, even after they are dead, as if the light stays in us even after life is gone and forgotten."

"You said you were with your son."

"He was twenty."

"And his mom?"

"She had already died."

"An illness?"

"She committed suicide."

"Don't joke with me."

"She stuck her head in the oven and turned on the gas. She was still young, and a poet, too. One of the best, at the peak of her creative power."

"Why then…?"

"Because of me. I met some other woman, we got together secretly for a while, then I simply left and moved in with her."

"And your wife killed herself."

"Not right away. We had two children. We still saw

each other. At times we lived together for a while, but her pride was hurt, she fell into depression, and was demanding help, my help. But I didn't see that or didn't want to see it. Then there were pills, sedatives, antidepressants. Then one day she stuck her head in the oven and left this world."

"You didn't feel guilty?"

"I don't want ever to be forgiven. If there's an eternity, I'm damned for all time. And that's just. But I've already received my punishment."

"What kind of punishment?"

"The woman I left my wife for and with whom I had a daughter, killed herself and our daughter in a moment of insanity. She couldn't bear me continually leaving and returning to her. She demanded we part, for good. When I refused, she killed herself."

"You know…"

"You've fallen in love with a monster."

"That's not it."

"That's exactly it. And now you'll be assailed by second thoughts. And when we get to your dream island, which will be soon, your infatuation will have died. You'll seek the first opportunity to go home."

"I just can't believe that all that happened."

"You wanted to know about my past."

"I can't believe that all that happened to you."

"Why? Because in fact I'm a small, average poet and only your infatuation's fantasy turned me into a great one?"

"That's not what I said, nor do I think that. I know you're a good poet, you enchant many people, and you enchanted me. But you're also a great poet, and I can't judge you, and I don't care. Something else bothers me."

"What?"

"Does it seem possible to you that poets' fates are so alike that they're almost identical?"

"That can't be ruled out. If we could check the fates of the passengers on this flight, we would find that in general terms they are stunningly alike. We're all people, subject to the same laws of possibility and probability."

"But not to such an extent that our fates would match in detail."

"Surely not."

"Then why does your story so remind me of the fate of one other poet?"

"I don't know."

"Was your first wife, the one who stuck her head in the gas oven, an American?"

"She was. How did you guess?"

"And you second wife, who also took your daughter to her death, was previously the wife of a Canadian poet?"

"You surprise me."

"The first was named Sylvia Plath, and the second Assia Wevill?"

"I see that you're more erudite than I thought."

"And your real name is Ted Hughes?"

"No, my real name is David Naylor, as you well know."

"Then why did you tell me the life story of Ted Hughes instead of your own?"

"Because it's more dramatic than mine and because mine is so boring that it would disappoint you."

"What disappoints me is that you didn't want to tell me your story, they way it really is. Even though I told you that I'm endlessly in love with you, you wanted to make an even greater impression on me. Why?"

"Will you believe me if I admit something?"

"I don't know any longer what I should believe."

"This time I'll be a hundred percent sincere. I have a pathological need not to be what I am. To be someone else."

"And why Ted Hughes of all people?"

"Not only him. Anyone who isn't me. Ted Hughes came up because our conversation touched on something—I don't know exactly what—that reminded me of him. And I slipped into his role."

"Then you're ill. Are you aware of that?"

"If that's illness, then it's very common. A real epidemic."

"But why would you want to be someone else? Is there anything wrong with being who you are?"

"There's nothing wrong with that on the face of it. Most people in the world have reconciled themselves to it. I'm one of those who haven't."

"Why not?"

"Because it's too much torture to be what and who you are twenty-four hours a day. Day after day, month after month, year after year. As if condemned to life in prison. Trapped in your story, in your fate, condemned to existing as always-the-same, without a chance to complain. Without a chance of becoming someone besides the one you are."

"All that is true, but why make a problem out of something that cannot be otherwise?"

"It can be. Not in actuality, but by play, by assuming roles that give you the sense of being another at least for a few moments."

"That kind of play is called dissimulating."

"Exactly. And as far as play goes, you're no less a master than I."

"What do you mean?"

"Didn't you tell me a half hour ago that you wanted to study literature?"

"Yes, and?"

"That you wanted to be a critic, review others' works, and thus show that you're smarter and more capable than them?"

"I did say that, but…"

"You also said that first you'd have to be capable of writing something better than what you're criticizing, and because you didn't want to lie and put on airs, you went to study anthropology instead."

"So what's the problem?"

"The problem, my dear, is that you don't study anthropology, but literature."

"How do you know?"

"I looked into it."

"You spied on me?"

"I wanted to know with whom I was going on a long trip."

"And now you know?"

"I didn't spy on you. You sent reviews of some poetry collections to a London journal where I work as an anonymous editor. Among them was a review of my last collection. You signed your real name. You added that you're finishing your literary studies and would like to use your knowledge to review contemporary literature."

"I never got a reply."

"Because you didn't deserve one. You can't find the door to enter poetry. You simply pasted theoretical statements about your knowledge onto the collections you reviewed. That's far too little. It's almost, as you said about me, a kind of illness."

"How did you know it was me?"

"You introduced yourself when you came up to me after my literary reading. I recalled the name. But you didn't know you were talking to the editor who had read your pieces. In one, you ended a review of my collection by saying that my poetic force had begun to fade."

"Forgive me."

"Yet after the literary reading, when you saw me in person, I suddenly became a great poet for you. You saw a handsome, sexy man who excited your female hormones. And suddenly poetry ceased to be so important. Which wasn't hard, because you never really understood it anyway."

"All that is true, but only half…"

"At this point, tears are probably in order, but they'll

be of no use."

"I'm so ashamed…"

"Things are what they are, and the dumbest thing would be for us to make that a problem."

"What then is left to us?"

"Sex on Bali. The amateur review hasn't yet got into bed with us. Or someone else's made up story. There's nothing but poetry in bed with us. Let's take advantage of that."

"Will we be able to, with this terrible feeling of shame and remorse?"

"I will just be one of the games we play, since we've been pretending the whole time to be who we're not."

"Why are we doing this?"

"We're people. We keep trying to pull ourselves up by our bootstraps."

"Are we the only two who do that?"

"I'm afraid not. If we were, the world would have a future."

"Can we do anything to guarantee it has a future?"

"No."

"Can we do anything for ourselves?"

"That's not a problem. A few nights and afternoons expending energy in bed in one of the beautiful Bali beach hotels, and everything that happened between us in this plane will sink into oblivion."

"That's hard for me to believe."

"Or it will remain with us as a reminder that as people we're flawed. Which would be invaluable."

"Do you still like me?"

"Is that important?"

"For me it is."

"I never really liked you. I can pretend that I do, but the question is whether you'll believe me. You never liked me either. Not really. You liked the feeling of being with me, a poet. You needed adventure. I did, too. Is anything wrong with that?"

8.

The Best Actor

"Don't be offended, but I can't believe what you said about Krishnamurti."

"I respect him a great deal. As a person. But not as a philosopher."

"Isn't it the same thing?"

"No. Socrates was one of the ugliest and most repulsive men in Athens, but his philosophy is the basis of Western civilization. Even a criminal can be a genius when he starts considering philosophic questions. And the reverse."

"Even though few people are aware of it."

"Oh, most people aren't aware of most things—especially, unfortunately, intellectuals, whose brains are deadened by narrowly defined fields into a few rigid categories. That might just be the problem of a great thinker like Krishnamurti."

"I don't understand."

"Look, he was a physically attractive, dignified, gray bearded wise man, as most people imagine him. He was interesting to listen to; he was pleasant, quick, and a splendid speaker. But after every lecture of his I was struck by the feeling of having obtained nothing."

"That's impossible."

"His problem was that he always talked about how important it was for us not to be conditioned, but he was one of the most conditioned people in the world. He couldn't free himself from his way of thinking or his rhetoric."

"Maybe his childhood memories prevented him."

"They shouldn't have. That's the first thing a spiritual person must overcome. I know that recurrences of childhood pains can be very powerful and often unconscious, but for a person to free the soul, they have to be conquered."

"If they can be found."

"Krishnamurti certainly found them. But he couldn't get rid of them. That's his tragedy. His thinking was caught in a vicious circle, constantly revolving around the question of existence, and in the end he got lost in abstractions."

"Nonetheless, he had a system…"

"He claimed he did. And he was very intolerant of people who didn't agree with his every thought. He was even intolerant of those who supported him. He was totally devoid of humor. And without a sense of humor it's impossible to achieve true wisdom."

"His wisdom was actually that he saw on every spiritual path, in every ideal, and in every faith an impediment tat should be avoided…"

"In the first place, that's impossible; in the second, it's not smart. It would have benefited him if he could have fathomed the thinking of other people, because it would have lent more breadth to his thoughts."

"That's true."

"In addition, there's the claim that 'No one influenced me!'" It's a sign of exaggerated self-confidence, a lack of humility, which isn't a move towards wisdom, but away from it. And he was unfortunately too enamored of himself and proud of being Krishnamurti."

"To some extent his admirers instilled that faith in him…"

"That means that he didn't deal decisively with his ego. He should have been respectful but heedless of admirers. He should have been thankful to people who *really* influenced his philosophy. But he couldn't recognize them."

"It is probably impossible to be completely

unconditioned..."

"And even less is it desirable. A wise man should admit: I am conditioned, but universally rather than locally. We're all conditioned, but most people are conditioned by a handful of local influences. Parents, peers, neighbors, education. That's bad. Wisdom begins when we admit that everything in the world conditions us, and therein is the gateway to freeing the soul."

"Absolutely everything in the world?"

"Of course. How are we served by suppressing consciousness of it? Avoiding any influences and denying conditioning is senseless, it is lying to oneself. And it's a contradiction, since life is a unity, and if we don't realize that, it becomes senseless and empty."

"Then we have to strive to be influenced by as many things as possible. To allow everything to penetrate our thoughts, accept everything..."

"Not necessarily accept. To allow things to come close and to check them. Not to reject them out of fear that they might uproot something that has already grown into a tree inside us, but to find room for new things in our mental space. And to accept them. It's truly sad that we reject the rigidity of the Christian faith and allow for evolution in our heads, while in our souls we fear it. I'm constantly surprised by that. A soul that doesn't allow for development is stunted."

"Some thinkers say that it's best to follow the tradition into which a person has been born..."

"To remain a Buddhist if you're a Buddhist, a Christian if you're a Christian, a Muslim if you're a Muslim, an atheist if you're an atheist, and an idiot if you're an idiot?"

"Soul and intellect are also subject to the laws of evolution, and can develop and change."

"Look around, take a look at the people sitting with us in the plane. Most are imprisoned. They're closed, locked up in their convictions, within the boundaries of their knowledge, within the boundaries of their prejudices, sympathies and antipathies. And hardly any of them are aware of it. Even fewer are looking for the key to escape their prison."

"In short, it's not good to follow just one search light, you have to follow a spectrum…"

"You have to remain fearlessly open, allow everything to come close, check everything, and only then choose. What kind of choice can there be if we have nothing to choose from?"

"But some squatting in their mental prisons think that they've already made a choice and that that is their choice."

"That form of mental illness, which we like to call common sense, is worst of all. This plane carries a crowd of spiritually dead people from one end of the world to the other."

"Maybe that's a slight exaggeration…"

"Being forgiving is a nice quality, but it doesn't necessarily have to conform with the facts."

"How many people on this plane would understand what we're talking about?"

"You understand me, and that's enough."

"I've read quite a few books, and Eastern philosophy is dear to me."

"There is only one philosophy. It can't be geographically defined. Geography, politics, and history are merely accessories. Something that strangles philosophy like a noose on the gallows. No matter where we live, we've all been dealing with the same questions for twenty centuries."

"In very different ways."

"Like every rooster crows his own way, but is still a rooster."

"The stewardess is coming with drinks. You want a glass of wine?"

"Whiskey. I only drink whiskey."

"Some in the West would find it hard to imagine an Indian wise man who enjoys alcohol."

"Where did you get the idea I'm an Indian wise man?"

"I don't know. Your appearance fits, we talked…"

"I'm a computer programmer by profession. I work in Silicon Valley, like a lot of Indians. I'm flying to Singapore via London to visit my brother, who lives there."

"Oh… It's been a long time since I've been so mistaken."

"But you're not. It's true I'm Indian. And a wise man as well. Just like you. Wisdom is our common quality, don't you think? The only problem is that we don't know how to share it."

***

"Staying with wisdom, doesn't it seem to you that everything revolves around the question of God's existence?"

"Oh, the world has changed so much that for some nowadays wisdom is a bad word, and God is a word atheists use to make fun of believers."

"That's true, but the question remains."

"That's not the biggest problem. The problem is that the question of God's existence determines our fate. And the fate of the world."

"Because the least intelligent among us seize the right to interpret what this or that sentence in one holy book or another means?"

"Let the adherent of a religion without criminal history cast the first stone."

"We had the Inquisition, we burned witches, exterminated tribes that believed in other gods, now we have terrorism, the Islamic State, slaughter of innocents, and idiocy as we've never seen. All in the name of God?"

"I'm afraid that as far as God goes, Hindus knew the answer three thousand years ago. Hindus are sincerely able to say, 'I am god,' and that's the end of the debate."

"My reason can only apprehend that as an absurdity."

"Because you can't break out of the prison of European Christian consciousness."

"Evidently not."

"By ceasing to distinguish between religions, ways of thinking, dogmas, and ideologies, including scientific ones, and combining them all in the declaration, 'I am god!'"

"No offense intended, but that still sounds absurd to me."

"Because historically your default consciousness is Christian. You have to set a different default."

"How?"

"I see you have a lot of questions, but you're not overly zealous in searching for answers."

"That's a sin that I gladly admit."

"Robert Paul Lanza."

"I don't understand."

"The American scientist who *Time* magazine named among the hundred most influential people in the world last year. He was a member of the team that was first in the world to clone a human embryo."

"Really?"

"He was also the first to clone a bison, and already twelve years ago a buffalo from the cell of an animal that died a quarter century before. I read that just today in *Time*. Don't you read the papers?"

"Too many, but I obviously missed that."

"However, he's not important because of cloning. His greatest achievement is a book in which he explains his theory of biocentrism. His theory is that life creates the universe, not the other way around."

"How is that possible?"

"Time and space don't exist. They are not objects but

only forms of sensory perception, mental constructs that help us apprehend the world. Time is subjective and dependent on consciousness."

"A courageous claim."

"Very courageous, because it disproves Einstein's theory of relativity. Among other things, Lanza said that if we separate consciousness from the world, reality ceases to exist."

"Interesting ideas. Too bad don't find the door into my consciousness."

"But they're close to the Indian way of thinking, which is close to the findings of the latest Western science."

"Maybe there will be a confluence in the end, and globalization will triumph in the sphere of consciousness as well."

"The biggest riddle is how it is possible that this process isn't already far behind us."

"I, too, am surprised it isn't."

"In the Jewish, Christian, and Muslim religions, God is a ruler, but at the same time a craftsman who created the world, which means the world is an invention, some mechanism made by an engineer. In India, the world isn't an invention, but a drama. Thus God isn't the architect of the world but a player who plays the world, all the roles at once, so each of us can say, 'I am god.' And each of us is a god, because we're one of the roles in the divine drama—one of the characters, a *persona*. *Persona*, as you know, means 'mask' in Latin, and the actors in Greek and Latin performances hid their faces behind masks in order to play what the mask represented. It's still that way today, even though the masks are mostly cosmetic. And thus we in fact wear masks of the god who in his drama, called the World, plays all possible roles."

"If we accept that as one of possible explanations."

"And why not? Wasn't it the Indians who first proved that the world started with a great explosion? First there was just God, who quickly became bored, and said to himself, 'This is unbearable, I have no one, I am only I, singular, I'm only One.' He exploded into the world from sadness and became everything that exists. He happily exclaimed, 'Now I'm no longer One, now I'm Many!'"

"That all sounds interesting, but…"

"…you can't believe that you're just one of the masks that God put on to act out his play."

"When I go to the theater, I'm aware that I'm watching a play and that what I'm watching isn't real…"

"Only if the performance is bad. If it isn't, you become immersed in it and share the experience. The only thing that perpetuates a dim awareness of watching a play is something the Germans call *Hintergedanken*, a sort of dim thought that remains far in the background of consciousness."

"The thought might be dim, but it's present."

"Not if the play is acted by the best actor, god, who knows how to perform all roles at once equally well and for an audience with an utmost desire to be convinced, because the audience, too, is god, and we along with the world are a series of masks with which god tries to convince us that he is not One but Many."

"But if that's true, why does god act such a cruel play? Death camps, beheadings of innocents, bombs falling on women and children, a plethora of injuries, hunger, unbearable pain, and deadly diseases. Doesn't that mean that god awards some and punishes others?"

"You're still in Christian default. If god plays all the roles, he suffers in the camp, is beheaded, a bomb falls on him—he is everything that happens in the drama entitled the World, including your doubt, because the drama is entitled the World and god plays it for fun, otherwise it wouldn't be complete."

"Interesting."

"Nothing new. Everything in the world is old and

eternal. It's a play that is continuously repeated in different costumes and with different props. Time isn't linear, as you Europeans think; time is circular, as we Indians believe."

"You have pointed out many things that I've never given a thought."

"And now you will?"

"Probably. You must be creating incredible things in Silicon Valley, given that you are so informed and so erudite."

"Useful, I'd say. There are few incredible things."

"Programs?"

"Programs, of course, and some other things."

"I know nothing about this, but can you let me in on what kind of things?"

"Yes, in view of the fact that you probably won't know what I'm talking about, and the whole thing will remain between us."

"By all means it will remain between us, there's no doubt about that."

"I create programs for breaking into computer systems of large corporations, banks, government organizations, and even governments themselves."

"Hacker programs?"

"I see you're familiar with the term."

"One sees newspaper reports."

"Then you know what my work is. Even though it's not mine. God is the one who creates programs through my brain and uses them to break into inaccessible regions of Himself, simply as a part of the game he calls the World. God loves games. In that regard, he's just like a child."

"But sometimes he, too, probably slips up."

"Never. He knows and sees everything, and if something goes wrong, he decides in advance that it will."

"Since god is perfect."

"Exactly so. And you? Why are you flying to Singapore?"

"Maybe you won't believe me, but I have to arrest god."

"I don't understand that."

"Or, if what you said is true, god has to arrest himself."

"Now I understand even less."

"The Chinese contact to whom you were going to sell your latest hacker program for five million dollars is already in jail. And you are awaited at the Singapore airport by five members of the crime squad."

"And who the hell are you?"

"Inspector William Rogers, Interpol."

9.

Key Vendors

"It's true we don't know each other," a middle-aged man turns to his neighbor, "but may I ask you something?"

"Of course."

"Have you read Orwell's *1984*?"

"Since I graduated, I read only newspapers."

"That's hard to believe."

"Really. Books are too thick and too much alike. No news. I want to know what's happening."

"Then I'm surprised you got on the plane without a newspaper."

"There wasn't time. The taxi got stuck in a traffic jam on the way to the airport. I barely caught the plane."

"If you read only newspapers, then you surely know what happened in Iraq some years ago."

"In Iraq? Something happens there every day."

"The bombs that the American government assured us precisely and humanely liberated the Iraqis right in their own homeland, on their ancestors' lands, fell on the city of Babylon."

"Ah, Babylon. Which gave translators so much work."

"Besides liberating seventy-seven people from the shackles of life, they apparently roused the souls of ancient times from their sleep."

"There's always a problem with souls, especially if you believe in them."

"Or some remnant of the Tower of Bable was hit that

had survived the Biblical punishment and was waiting there unnoticed until the moment that one of the smart bombs of a brave new civilization liberated it."

"I vaguely recall a report about that."

"Then you also know that something unusual happened."

"Can you be more specific?"

"I'm talking about the changes that happened to language as a means of communication."

"Aha…"

"Things are unexpectedly no longer what they are, but often their opposites."

"Really?"

"If you send half a million soldiers to attack a sovereign state, you could at least admit that you're trying to occupy Iraqi cities. Why is it necessary to lie that you are liberating them?"

"We?"

"Aren't you an American?"

"I didn't send anyone to Iraq. I sell electronic keys."

"There was a time when we called people who fought against occupiers of their land patriots, freedom fighters, defenders of the homeland."

"Which is quite right."

"In the Iraq war, patriots were those attacking. The defenders were described as the enemy, who was prepared to kill the freedom loving Americans in order to keep a dictator in power."

"It's a warped world."

"The Iraqis were faulted for not respecting the rules of war. Rules that the aggressor set.

"Look…"

"Maybe we should reclassify defending one's homeland as a war crime!"

"Well, I…"

"I watch and read about that and similar things and

am surprised. Not so much by what is happening, but by the metamorphosis of language that we're witnessing. And I ask myself whether this is something new or have we simply forgotten what language really is."

"It's not new."

"How do you know?"

"Didn't Oliver Goldsmith write that the actual aim of language is not to express our desires but to hide them?"

"Wait… you said you don't read books."

"Mark Twain said that lying is universal—we all lie, we all have to lie. It follows that we have to learn to lie thoughtfully and circumspectly, with good intentions, and not for our own benefit, but for others'; we have to behave with healing kindness, humanely, not cruelly and maliciously… we have to lie forcefully, openly, and with our heads held high, not hesitantly and apprehensively, as if ashamed of our calling."

"Why didn't you tell me?"

"That I read books? I was interested in your reaction."

"We have more in common than I thought."

"Much more."

"But if it's the way Mark Twain says, lying is the only truth of language. And language is one of the most fearsome weapons of mass destruction."

"Because of the ambiguous, poetic, myth building power it bears, it can't be otherwise. Dark and light coexist in all layers of creation."

"How right you are! In the end, every literary work is a lie, a fruit of imagination."

"Language, which is a two-edged sword in fumbling hands and a deadly weapon in the mouths of the avaricious, is also a risky path leading to a semblance of truth. Of real truth, which must, in order to remain truth, never be enthroned."

"Even though the American priest on an American

aircraft carrier was not talking about such truth when he declared, I quote, 'It's a just war, because it is waged against everything that opposes peace."

"A real marvel of language."

"You're probably too young to remember the Vietnam War."

"I was a child."

"The American government at the time was going through a similar phase of poetic creativity. The war was never a war at all, but always just an international armed conflict. Constant air raids became a routine defensive reaction of limited engagement. Erroneous bombing of friendly villages was navigational misdirection."

"As Humpty Dumpty said, 'When I say a word, its meaning is what I choose for it—nothing more, nothing less.'"

"Unusual."

"What?"

"That we judged each other so wrongly."

"But we didn't. We're both writers, both flying to Australia to an international festival at the central aboriginal reservation, we both used some small lies to determine who we're sitting next to."

"How did you figure that out?"

"I became suspicious right at the start."

"But you said you don't read books."

"And you thought I was an American."

"You're not?"

"Canadian. Toronto. The accent threw you off."

"But you really sell electronic keys?"

"Is that an unsuitable occupation for a writer?"

"No, no... After all, Faulkner sold stamps."

"And what do you do?"

"You won't believe it. I sell electronic keys."

"I thought that lying was over."

"Really. I work for Siemens in Vienna. I travel all

over the world. I'm always on the road. Long flights and being stuck in hotel rooms afford me just enough free time to publish a short novel every year."

"And what's your name?"

"Let's leave that for later. Lunch is coming. What will you have, fish or chicken?"

***

"Hard to believe, isn't it? That two writers flying to the same event find themselves sitting next to each another."

"And they both make a living selling electronic keys."

"If the story turned up in a novel, most readers would say that it stretches the bounds of credibility."

"True. Anything can happen in life, but in literature, only what is permitted."

"Except when some author allows himself something new."

"I assume that we both know what the critics have said about the most well-known literary works."

"Tolstoy on Baudelaire's *Fleur du Mal*: The collection contains not one poem that is clear and can be understood without a certain effort – an effort seldom rewarded, for the feelings which the poet transmits are evil and very low ones."

"A genius about a genius."

"Exactly."

"Milton Schulman on Beckett: *Waiting for Godot* is another of those plays that try to lift superficiality to significance through obscurity. It should please those who prefer to have their clichés masquerading as epigrams."

"And when Schulman was asked twenty years later how he could have been so wrong, he lost his temper: We didn't know then what we were watching!"

"Depressing."

"The *Edinburgh Review* on Byron: We advise him immediately to give up his involvement with poetry... we hope this is the last thing we will receive from this young man, who is in the best instance an intruder in the vineyards of Parnassus."

"Vladimir Nabokov on Joseph Conrad: I cannot abide Conrad's souvenir shop style, bottled ships and shell necklaces of romantic clichés."

"George Orwell on Dickens: It is because Dickens' characters have no mental life... Dickens is able to reach simply people, which Tolstoy is not."

"An anonymous critic on Eliot's *The Waste Land*: Fanciful patchwork of parodies and learned borrowings."

"The *New Statesman* on the same book: Unintelligible, the borrowings cheap and the notes useless."

"And one of the worst—H.L. Mencken on Henry James: ... an idiot, and a Boston idiot to boot, than which there is nothing lower in the world..."

"What about this one—Chesterton on Joyce: ... Joyce is rather inaudible, because he is talking to himself..."

"Joseph Conrad on D.H. Lawrence: Filth. Nothing but obscenities."

"We could go on forever."

"Why? Isn't it clear that literature has nothing more to say to us?"

"I wouldn't agree. Because then we, too, would have to quit."

"I will. Maybe I already have."

"Isn't it strange that we're writers but haven't heard of each another?"

"There're too many of us."

"Are too many books? Too many stories?"

"Both. All stories were told long ago."

"And now we're just repeating them? Each in his own way, each in his own style, but in essence they're the same, without noticeable originality?"

"What are the themes that we've been writing about for three thousand years?"

"Human relationships? Pride? Humility? Punishment for the former and the latter? Infatuation with pleasures? Betrayal, infidelity? Loyalty and the punishment that follows? A life of lies? Search for one's essence? Tales of wandering? Tales of contemporary problems?"

"Rewrites of nineteenth-century novels? A hundred variations on *Anna Karenina*? A hundred variations on the *Odyssey*? Variations on variations? Stories about whatever comes to the author's mind?"

"Is originality in literature even possible anymore?"

"Only by stumbling into it. And that's what we're all waiting for."

"Although that's not the worst thing."

"No?"

"The worst thing is that there are more and more books in the world and ever less people prepared to read them."

"And out of those who still read, there are continually less who know how to read."

"Reading is supposed to be a pleasure, not a strain."

"The book is an attack to our sensibility, and reading ought to be surrender."

"We open up and wait for an orgasm."

"If we don't get one, we usually blame the author. He wasn't penetrating enough, he didn't excite us enough."

"Who knows any more that reading is a game for two? And that the quality of the game depends not only on the author, but on the reader as well?"

"Exactly. Each of us has a different range of knowledge, experiences, and memories. In each of us a literary work plays a different melody."

"And not always the same one. It can be different at a second reading."

"Umberto Eco saw in a literary a machine for

generating interpretations."

"On the shelf a book is a dead object, it only comes alive when you open it."

"At times it seems to me that only children still realize that."

"That's true. Only children still know how to read innocently, to get into a book and live it, to add their interpretation to it."

"I'm afraid that most adults lost the ability to read creatively in high school. If not there, then at the university for sure, where reading is studying, copying, and defining."

"What did you study?"

"Anthropology. Which I didn't finish. And you?"

"You won't laugh?"

"I promise."

"Art history. Which I didn't finish either."

"You know what the problem is? Scientific and technical culture has robbed us of the spontaneity necessary for experiencing. We truly no longer even know how to experience our own experiences. At times I have the feeling that life is passing me by and all I can do is waive at it. Of course, it never waives back."

"The same goes for reading. Most people engage in it while fitted with some straightjacket of deeply ingrained opinions into which they try to stuff the book in order to tame it."

"That's true. Even if we imagine that we're reading out of a desire for an experience that might renew us, most often we're only looking for affirmation of our suppositions and prejudices."

"Just as we always think that only advice we want to hear is good advice."

"It's terrible to have to live in such times."

"We're so used to definitions that we trust only what is branded with a known label, with which experts convey what we can expect from the contents."

"Experts, people we expect to think for us."

"We've built most definitions into our psychodynamics, and we like to call automated reactions to what we read an aesthetic sense."

"Of course, we're convinced that we know what beauty is, what is special, what is meaningful, and what a literary work's role is. At a certain stage of mental development we no longer admit that these things are subjective and relative."

"We try to dam a river to make a lake, and literature to produce knowledge."

"That's why we usually quarrel with every book we take up from the first page on."

"You and I do?"

"Well… to be honest, me, too. Not always, but often enough."

"The same thing happens with me."

"For a long time I thought that reading enriches the soul and hones the sensibilities, but doesn't react to challenges that threaten to destroy my picture of the world, which gives me a modicum of security."

"You no longer think that?"

"I still do. But I'm increasingly filled with doubts."

"And what sort of books do you write, if I may ask?"

"Short stories, novels, essays. Crime stories, too. After all, even James Joyce read them."

"Although after his death, his wife burned every last one of them."

"Then people still believed in a difference between high and low literature. What about you?"

"It's hard to say. I only write novels. Mostly romances. That's the one thing that readers, for the most part female readers, still buy."

"And? Are you successful?"

"Don't forget that I make a living selling electronic keys."

"Just like me. Even though at least my crime books sell relatively well. To be honest—and I don't mean to brag—a little while ago on the way to the restroom, I noticed one of the passengers reading my novel *A Bomb on a Plane*. Poor choice for a flight, but whatever. The fellow is probably a masochist."

"I'm surprised he hasn't yet caused panic, to be followed by a forced landing and his arrest."

"Oh, the book is just a book, something trivial. Even the flight attendants know that."

"In short, we're not best-selling writers."

"Maybe you are. May I ask what your name is?"

"Trevor Morris."

"Unfortunately I have to admit that I haven't heard of you."

"What can you do? There're too many writers. And yours?"

"Nigel Rodgers."

"I, too, have to admit that the name isn't familiar."

"That's precisely the problem. A name, a trademark, sells books, not their quality."

"That's for sure."

"Not long ago Stephen King sent his newest work under an invented name to ten publishers and also to his usual one."

"And?"

"Four of the ten didn't even answer, five declined the promising but amateur text, and only one replied that it might include it in their plans, but only after substantial revisions. His own publisher, which has earned millions with King's works, didn't even realize it was his."

"Years ago, the late Nobel laureate Doris Lessing did something similar."

"Smart editors just abound in the field of publishing."

"Yet one thing doesn't add up for me."

"No?"

"How is it that the two of us, relatively unknown authors, financially by no means successful enough to survive without a job, were invited to an aboriginal festival in Australia?"

"I wrote a short story about aborigines that was published in some Australian journal."

"And I wrote a travelogue about a trip across northern Australia, in which I also described meetings with aborigines."

"There we have the answer."

"Interesting criteria."

"Nothing literary."

"But there's something that bothers me more than what we've been talking about."

"That is?"

"How is it that we both make a living selling electronic keys?"

"That would be too great a coincidence, no?"

"Possible somehow, yet extraordinary."

"I have to admit that I told a lie. Now that we're better acquainted, it's almost my duty to apologize."

"I'm listening."

"I don't sell keys. I'm a professor of art history at the University of London. But as a writer, like you, I'm far from having my picture appear in the papers."

"All along I had the feeling it would be something like that."

"It's possible that you don't sell electronic keys either. Can you share what you really do?"

"In fact I really do sell electronic keys. My childhood dream of traveling the world at others' expense came true for me."

"And now you're happy."

"I'd be pressed to say I'm not. And you?"

"I can't say that I am."

"It's really too bad we can't live off our writing."

"Our only comfort is that we are far from being the only ones."

"We started out badly and are ending well."

"On the contrary. We started well, in the spirit of an argument that was actually a conversation, a dialog. And we're ending with calm agreement that we live in times when writers are merely oddballs."

"But electronic keys have at least symbolic meaning."

"I don't understand."

"You sell people keys to doors that lead into the world of literature."

"Most are quite happy if they can get into their hotel room without a problem."

"And what do they find in the bedside drawer?"

"The Bible."

10.
Competition of Quotomaniacs

"How pleasant it is to do nothing and then rest," the young man by the window wakes up from napping.

"That's right, it's high time we start memorizing," a somewhat younger man in the middle seat reminds him.

"Right now?"

"There's not much time, and you know yourself we didn't practice enough."

"What do you suggest?"

"We could start with A and go through the alphabet."

"We've done that too many times. Let's do it by chance, randomly."

"Don't be afraid of your enemies. The worst they can do is to kill you. And don't be afraid of your friends. The worst they can do is to betray you."

"Be afraid of those who do not kill or betray, but because of whose silence betrayal and killing exist."

"Imagination is intelligence with an erection."

"It's not important what you do in life, but it's very important that you do it."

"Nothing that you find in small print is good news."

"As far as women go, their intelligence is boundless – until you ask them to be coherent."

"Only one thing is important in art: the part that cannot be explained."

"A banker is a person who is willing to make you a loan if you present sufficient evidence to show you don't need it."

"I don't think anybody should write his autobiography until after he is dead."

"Day after day people are straying away from church and going back to God."

"Do you think that the fate of this flight is in God's hands?"

"Wait... who said that?"

"I did."

"Can we stop?"

"Let's. For a bit. My brain is twisted into a wad of spaghetti."

"The competition will go on a lot longer."

"I know. I hope we sleep well beforehand."

"It would be good to practice as often and as much as possible. This is the first time we're taking part. We don't know what the whole thing will be like."

"As it is we don't have a chance of winning."

"That's for sure, with your defeatist attitude."

"It's not about that. Have you ever heard of plain exhaustion?"

"You need another beer. Then we can continue."

"I don't remember anything anymore."

"Just a little. Let's finish with religion."

"All religions are founded on the fear of the many and the cleverness of the few."

"We must respect the other fellow's religion, but only in the sense and to the extent that we respect his theory that his wife is beautiful and his children smart."

"Science tells us how the heavens go. Religion tells us how to go to haven."

"The religion of one age is the literary entertainment of the next."

"The whole religious complexion of the modern world is due to the absence from Jerusalem of a lunatic asylum."

"Can we stop there? That's a good conclusion."

"Right. Shall we continue in half an hour?"

"An hour?"

"As long as you don't disappoint me in the end."

"We can only avoid that by me disappointing you right now by refusing to cooperate."

"You know it's a competition of pairs, so why are you suddenly threatening me?"

"You're turning me into a slave of your ambitions."

"I thought they were shared ambitions. Why then are we flying to Australia?"

"I won't torpedo our goals. Your impatience will."

"I'm sorry. I also have moments when my brain automatically shuts down. I'll wait. I only ask that you don't leave me in the lurch."

"And if I do? Will you retaliate?"

"Before deciding to retaliate, dig two graves, says an old Chinese proverb."

"Right. Rest time."

***

A few minutes later, the elegant lady on the aisle turns to them and asks, "Excuse me, young men. Are you by any chance professors?"

"Why?" asks the one sitting next to her.

"I couldn't help but overhear your conversation. You were talking very loudly."

"Our sincere apologies."

"No, no. I heard a great deal of wisdom."

"Wisdom was once a rarity, ma'am, connected with Socrates and people like him. If today you google the word 'wisdom,' you'll get 270,000,000 results."

"You probably teach at some university."

"No, ma'am, we're failed students who would like to accomplish at least something in life."

"And what's that?"

"We'd like to win an international quotations championship in Brisbane."

"You're quotation aficionados?"

"Yes, people with such good memory that we can memorize most utterances by famous people and connect them in a meaningful, narrative whole."

"Based on what I heard, you'll win."

"Thank you, ma'am."

"I have no doubt whatsoever."

"'Doubt that encompasses everything, ceases to be doubt.' Wittgenstein."

"Very smart. I'm a simple woman who likes to read. And I love dogs. I have three. Different ones. A husky, a St. Bernard, and a poodle. And I often wonder whether the first two, which are big, aren't asking if the poodle doesn't belong to some strange religious cult."

"Ma'am, are you aware that you're repeating something that Rita Rudner first said?"

"Who's Rita Rudner?"

"We don't know. With few exceptions, we only memorize quotes, not their authors."

"After all they are not important."

"Have you ever gone from one room to another, ma'am, without knowing why?"

"Quite often."

"Well, that's how dogs spend their lives."

"Maybe so," replies the lady. "I often recognize something that reminds me of a strange loathing in my dogs' eyes, as if they had suddenly decided that all people are idiots."

"Do you know who said that? John Steinbeck!"

"Who would have thought."

"Maybe you should go to the competition with us."

"Unfortunately I can't, because I'm flying to Australia for another reason. The doctors told me I have only three months to live. I'm an Australian, although I've been living in London for years. I'd like to die in the land where I was born. In the house where I was born. In a small village. And I'd like to be buried there, in the village cemetery. In the same plot as my parents, brother, and sister."

The two young men exchange glances and are silent.

"Did any one of the great men or women you quote say something about that?"

"Quite a few."

"Can you tell me?"

"Death is a very dull, dreary affair, and my advice to you is to have nothing whatsoever to do with it." Somerset Maugham."

"Life is a great surprise. I do not see why death should not be an even greater one." Nabokov.

"What is philosophy but study of death?"

"Socrates?" the lady asks.

The two young men are quiet for a while.

"Are you going to the Brisbane competition, too?" asks the one sitting next to her.

"How did you guess?" the lady asks in surprise.

"The story about how you want to die in your home village wasn't very convincing."

"I know. But I like to tell it to someone on almost every flight."

"To be honest, I suspected you to be a competitor of ours."

"Actually I'm not. I'll take part in a special section of the competition."

"We didn't know one exists."

"I'm surprised. After all it was announced."

"Did you hear anything about it?" one turns to the other.

"Nothing of the sort. What is the special section of the competition?"

"You have to guess the source of well known sayings and their variants."

"You mean..."

"Better a sparrow in hand than a dove on the roof. Things like that."

"But why isn't there any information on this?"

"I received an invitation in the mail. Maybe because I took part in the competition three years ago, and they sent the invitation to everyone they had on their list."

"Everyone should have been allowed to register."

"I don't know how it works, but I registered in the hope of moving up from third to first place this time."

"You were in third place? Then you have to be exceptionally good."

"But there aren't as many such sayings as there are quotations," says the young man by the window, "it's a lot easier. If it's not too late, I'd sign up, too. Do you think it's too late?"

"I wouldn't know," answers the lady. "But do you really think it's easier?"

"It has to be."

"We can test it. At least we won't be bored."

"Right here on the plane?"

"Why not?" says the young man in the middle. "All the world's a stage and we're merely players."

"We can start with that," proposes the lady.

"A bit too easy," replies the young man by the window. "Shakespeare, Jaques' monolog, act 2 of *As You Like It*."

"And what did he mean by that?" asks the lady.

"Is that part of the game?" inquires the young man in the middle.

"That's the essence of the game. We all know these hackneyed phrases. Just citing them isn't a competition."

"I don't understand."

"The essence of the game is finding the best answer to the question of what the saying means and who said something similar. For example, a Spanish proverb goes, We see the face but don't know the heart."

"Interesting," says the young man by the window, "only too bad I don't see how that ties in with Shakespeare's words."

"Didn't you just say that the world is nothing but a play?"

"I did and I stick by it."

"Horace Walpole described the world as a comedy for thinking people and a tragedy for those who feel," says the lady. "It's question of to what extent and how often we play roles. Are all of us really actors?"

"There are times I'm almost convinced that we are," says the young man by the window. "At times it seems the chasm between what I feel I really am and the mask I have to put on in order to take part in life is too wide."

"Then we've arrived at the essence of the game."

"But ma'am," says the young man in the middle, "It's true we can imagine having to put on a mask when we go to work and in public. When we try to be social or find a partner. Or when we apply ourselves to playing a role our family expects, for example. But that means that there's a difference between our character and the way we are while playing a role."

"Exactly," says the young man by the window. "And if we're all perpetually playing, doesn't that mean we're perpetually just our own game? The mask that doesn't hide anything and is never taken off is no longer a mask. It becomes a face."

"That's exactly why we have to choose the roles we play in life carefully," says the lady.

"I'm curious," says the young man in the middle, "how many metaphors for life we find in theater."

"And what roles are we three playing at the moment?" asks the lady.

"Hmm," says the boy by the window.

"It's a little to early to think about that," says the

young man in the middle.

"I agree," says the lady. "After all, we've hardly begun. Let's say that in this case there's no winner. Now let's go on."

"You?" asks the young man in the middle.

"I'll go," says the young man by the window. "'The only certainty is that nothing is certain.' Who said that, ma'am?"

"Pliny the Elder, a Roman who lived between 23 and 79 C.E."

"Bravo! And in what connection did he say those words?"

"I think it was in connection with God. In his *Natural History*."

"In fact he was trying to say that we can live in peace even if we're not a hundred percent sure of anything."

"We have to be about some things…"

"He was, too. For example, about turtle shell shavings being a strong aphrodisiac. He only talked about uncertainty in connection with God. That it's impossible to prove whether He exists. And that we can live in peace with that."

"But if we firmly believe something, that influences our life," says the young man in the middle. "If I believe in God, I'll act differently than if I'm convinced he doesn't exist."

"If there's no certainty, we can rely on probability. What is more probable—that God exists or not? Here the entirety of human knowledge over the last three thousand years opens up before us. None of us, no one in the world could match it. We can only guess."

"It's true that nothing is certain, yet some things are more certain than others."

"Death and taxes?"

"It's less certain that one of us will win this game."

"Why?"

"Because we don't have a system. Without agreeing on scoring that we all approve."

"That's right, first we should make rules."

"You've taken part in this kind of competition, ma'am. You know the rules."

"We set rules in order to break them."

"But not in competitions."

"Especially there. Isn't everything in life a competition? For a place in a good school, for a good partner, for our children's success in school, for a well paying job? For victory at the world championship of quotation aficionados?"

"But they do have rules there. Just like in sports."

"Where a third of the participants are helped to victory by taking illegal drugs?"

"Wait, wait," says the young man by the window. "We're off topic."

"When one door closes, another opens."

"Better the devil you know…"

"More tears are shed over answered prayers than unanswered ones."

"Don't fix it if it's not broken."

"The road to hell is paved with good intentions."

"And that's the road we're on. We're playing a game that's not a real game, because it doesn't have rules. It didn't come to any of us to agree on them before starting. We're competing for a prize that no one can win, because there's no jury. We think we're smart, but in fact all we have is a good memory. At the competition we're planning to attend, first prize will go to a tape recorder."

"They don't exist anymore. New inventions replaced them."

"What kind of competition do you actually plan to take part in, ma'am?"

"None. I invented the whole thing."

"That's what I thought. Why?"

"I wanted to prove to you that you're not that smart."

"We're probably not, but why did you want to prove it?"

"Because you don't seem to be aware of that."

"Right, you mentioned that. But what use is that to us?"

"Perhaps you'll remember that the smallest thing in the world can be explained in a thousand ways. And that not one of them is better than another. And that by far the worst is their sum."

"I wish I could understand that."

"A person travels the world to find what he needs, and when he returns, he finds it at home."

"Or not. He might not travel to find anything but to distance himself from what he has."

"Is that your reason for participating in the world championship of quotation aficionados?"

"I don't understand," says the young man by the window.

"I don't either," says the young man in the middle.

"In each of us there's a tiny seed from which wisdom can burst forth. But that frightens us, so we go to school and cover the seed with other people's knowledge. That's why we memorize a thousand quotations and set off to the other end of the world to prove—more to ourselves than to others—that we're educated. And the seed of wisdom slowly dies under the weight of others' knowledge. And then, despite all our intelligence, we're stupid."

"Can I ask you something?"

"Please do."

"Who are you really?"

"A passenger on flight 2191 from London to Singapore and then on to Australia."

"So are we."

"That's how they'll describe us if the plane plunges into the ocean in the next several hours. That's unlikely but not to be ruled out. And what can't be ruled out can happen."

"But who are you in reality?"

"Reality? Are any of the passengers on this plane, including the crew, real?"

"I'm afraid that in a minute I'm going to drop out of this conversation."

"That's alright. Aren't all three of us excluded from most of the conversations on this plane? Not to mention all the other planes in the air. Something over six thousand said a gentleman two rows back. Someone else said twice as many. Not to mention all the other conversations in the world from which we've been and always will be excluded. And in the end we'll be excluded from all conversations. Will the din of stupidity in the world diminish because of that?"

"To tell the truth, I'm a little afraid of you."

"That's a good thing. After all, I could be your mother."

"By age, for sure. Otherwise, I don't have a mother."

"Did she die?"

"No, she disappeared when I was ten."

"Just disappeared?"

"Vanished. Into thin air."

"With a man who wasn't your father?"

"That would be too ordinary for her. She was an artist, a famous painter, and she valued herself enough not to stoop to clichés."

"Then she really did vanish."

"Every two years I received a letter from her, so she would know what was going on with me, keep up with my education, check I was on the proper path, and say I have to forget about her so it would be easier for me."

"And is it?"

"No. I felt worse with every letter she sent. Until something snapped and I had to be treated."

"Successfully?"

"I think so. I blamed my father for her disappearance and I've been fine since then."

"And you father?"

"I don't live with him. I never visit. I'm a high school teacher, and that's enough for me."

"But you think about your mom sometimes? About where she could be, what she might be doing, and why she disappeared?"

"For a long time I did. And then her letters stopped coming and I forgot about her."

"Completely?"

"No, I still remember her and—though it sounds strange—I miss her. And a few months ago I received another letter from her. She informed me it was her last."

"Did she give a reason?"

"That I am an adult now, and independent, so I don't need her any more."

"But she wasn't there when you *did* need her."

"No, she wasn't there."

"You'll probably never forgive her for abandoning you. And your father."

"My father took care of himself quickly, but it was hard for me. For a very long time. But now I've accepted it as a fact of life. And I live. More or less normally. I expected more from myself, but what I have isn't bad. And this kind of competition is a comfort. It's like a promise that I can achieve more than life intended for me."

"What would you say to your mom if you were to meet her?"

"That's not possible, but if I did, I would say, 'Mom, are you really my mom?"

"And if she said yes, would you demand proof?"

"Why? If she said she's my mom, she surely is. And I'd simply hug her."

"Do you hold it against her for vanishing?"

"After all these years? No. She must have had a

reason."

"We all have reasons for doing what we do. But some reasons are good and others are bad. If you found that her reason was bad, would you still love her?"

"But I do. Even though it doesn't help me."

"Why not?"

"Because she's gone."

"And if she ever returned, would things change?" asks the lady after a long silence.

"She doesn't exist for me as a person anymore, but only as pain that she caused me."

"Can you live with that pain?"

"Some people have to live with arthritis, a tooth ache, or migraines."

"But the pain caused by a mother that abandoned you is surely worse."

"I don't like talking about it."

"I'm curious because something like that happened to me."

"Your mom vanished when you were ten?"

"No. I'm a mom and I abandoned my son when he was ten. Twelve, to be exact, but it's not a big difference."

"Why?"

"I think I was too young, unstable, self-centered, and too little in love with the boy's father. And too much in love with someone else. Who in the end was a great disappointment."

"Life is a moderately good play with a badly written third act," says the young man sitting next to the lady.

"Truman Capote," says the lady.

"We're born, we eat potatoes, then we die," says the young man by the window.

"Where's that from?" the lady and young man in the middle ask in unison.

"A proverb from Easter Island."

"And that's the truth," says the lady. "Perhaps we're

too conceited if we expect more."

"Should we practice some more?" asks the young man by the window. "Given that we're going to a competition?"

"About life?"

"Why not, since that's all we have."

"How did I come into the world? Why was I not consulted? And if I am compelled to take part in it, where is the director? I want to see him."

"Kierkegaard."

"Life is a public performance on the violin, in which you must learn the instrument as you go along."

"E.M. Forster."

"Have you noticed that life, real honest to goodness life, with murders, catastrophes, and fabulous inheritances takes places almost exclusively in newspapers?"

"Anouilh."

"What an awful thing life is. It's like soup with lots of hairs floating on the surface. You eat it nonetheless."

"Flaubert."

"May I suggest something else?" asks the lady. "Part of my competition also involves knowledge of how many geniuses flunked out of school."

"Really? How do you know?"

"I inquired."

"Even though you're not taking part in the competition?"

"Maybe I will."

"We don't feel at all comfortable with that subject," says the young man by the window.

"Well, we could try," says the young man sitting next to her.

"Fine," says the young man by the window.

"Who left the University of Edinburgh as a failed student of medicine," continues the lady, "and was then bored to death for some time at Cambridge University?"

"Winston Churchill?" offers the young man by the window.

"No. Finally his interest in natural history secured him a bunk on *The Beagle*."

"Charles Darwin!" both young men exclaim at once.

"How about this one," the lady continues. "His parents were afraid that their son was retarded, because until the age of nine he spoke haltingly and answered questions only after thinking a long time. He performed so poorly in high school that a teacher advised him to quit, because it was as plain as day he would never accomplish anything in life. He didn't pass the entrance exams at the University of Zürich on his first try…"

"Albert Einstein!" exclaims the young man next to her.

"Excellent!" the lady squeezes his elbow encouragingly.

"I have an example like that," says the young man by the window.

"Well, go on," says his companion.

"Even though his mom drove him to learn as much as possible so that people wouldn't think him an ass, the son did so poorly in a Franciscan school, especially in German grammar, that the mom couldn't have been more disappointed. Neither was he able to correctly decline words in French, Latin, or Greek…"

"Heinrich Heine," says the lady, "one of the greatest German poets."

"Isn't that great comfort for us, not having achieved anything significant at our age?" says the young man next to her.

"One more example, then we'll quit," says the lady. "The third child in a family, all of whose members had achieved great success, was so down that his mother withdrew him from Eton to save tuition for his younger brother. He was apprenticed to some attorney, but mostly looked out the window. The distraught mother sent him to a military school, seeing as how he was only good to be turned into cannon fodder. Years later, this dullard led the British army to defeat Napoleon at the Battle of Waterloo…"

"Duke of Wellington!" both young men exclaimed at once.

"Bravo," says the lady. "I'm sure you'll reach the top at the competition in Brisbane."

"And you, too," says the young man next to her.

"If I decide to go."

"You have to. That's why you're flying to Australia, isn't it?"

"I've never been clear about my goals in life."

"Can I ask you something?" says the boy next to her.

"Please do."

"Something personal?"

"It's high time we're done with being quotation aficionados."

"Since my mom vanished when I was ten, I'm curious as to why you abandoned your twelve-year old son."

"Why does the interest you?"

"It might help me understand why my mom disappeared literally overnight, with no warning."

"Not all such cases are alike."

"But if two mothers suddenly leave their children, the reasons must be at least somewhat similar."

"As I said, another man was to blame. In love with theater and film, young, and inexperienced, I saw in him an object of desire that I couldn't resist. He was exceptionally attractive, spirited, and talkative—the exact opposite of my husband, who was attentive but the personification of boredom."

"But the child surely meant something to you."

"As I said, the actor completely turned my head. He kept talking about how he was one step from being a

Hollywood star, and then, he said, we would both be famous. I was stupid enough to want that and I believed him."

"And did your wish come true?"

"If it did, would I be sitting on this plane, a lonely old woman full of bitterness?"

"And you just left, without thinking about the child?"

"Not at all. At first I insisted on taking the child with me. But my husband wouldn't give him up just like that. He would have demanded custody, we would have been in court for years, and I didn't have the strength for something like that. Besides, the actor I'd fallen for didn't want me and a child. He had even sent his two to an orphanage. Their mom had died several years before. The simple truth was that we wanted to be free. Both of us. To begin a new life."

"I assume it didn't quite work out."

"For several years it seemed heavenly. Then it became clear that in fact he was a very mediocre actor. He came to the same conclusion and started drinking. I was to blame for everything. It came to a point when we were arguing day and night. And then he did what I had done to my own son. He disappeared overnight."

"But it shouldn't be too hard to find an actor, even if he's not a star."

"The whole time we were traveling between England, Australia, the U.S., and Canada. He went to auditions all over the world in order to get roles in which he had to do something more than beat someone up, serve coffee, fire a machine gun, or drive a taxi. Where was I to find him? Perhaps I could have, but it was over for me."

"During that time, did you ever think of the son you had abandoned?"

"He was always on my mind."

"Didn't you ever have the urge to look for him?"

"His father had found a partner, my son was living in a more or less stable family, and I didn't have a right to interfere. But from afar I kept track of his progress in school and to an occupation."

"Did you ever write to him?"

"Quite a few times. But without a return address for him to answer. I was afraid he wouldn't. That he would refuse. That he would write, 'Thanks for all the long years without you.' I reconciled myself to the pain. He probably did, too."

"My mom wrote to me, too. I wouldn't have refused to answer. I've missed her my whole life. Had she written an address, I wouldn't have hesitated for a minute. I would have searched for her right away.

"Would you even have recognized her?"

"Of course."

"It's hard for a ten-year old child to remember the faces of people twenty years later. Would he remember grade school classmates? Besides, his mom had aged in that time. She would be different."

"Not so different that he wouldn't recognize her."

"My son wouldn't have a clue who I was if I suddenly appeared before him. And I would never dare say I'm his mom. I wouldn't want him to be completely disappointed in me. He was disappointed his whole life. I'd like to preserve at least the illusion that he wouldn't reject me if we were to meet."

"Do you think my mom looks at it the same way?"

"She surely follows your life from a distance and is pleased with it."

"But I'm not. Why doesn't she want to give me an address?"

"Perhaps because after twenty years a meeting would cause emotional distress not only in her life, but in yours as well."

"Isn't she aware that a meeting would bring both of us forgiveness, happiness, and a new life?"

"That's how you imagine it. You're still young. She has more experience and probably knows that the reality would be different."

"It's odd how many similar stories there are in the world."

"I don't at all envy writers who must labor to think up new ones."

"They don't actually have to," says the young man by the window. "The Italian Gozzi wrote a book a good two hundred years ago about how there are only thirty-six possible dramatic plots, and he listed all of the works that existed in as many categories."

"Maybe some things have changed since then," observes the lady.

"Not much," says the boy by the window. "The atom bomb, a story about the end of the world, remote control, a story about mental breakdown, smart phone, story about escape from reality."

"I still have hope," says the lady. "I'll go to the competition with you. I won't take part, but I'd like to see which one of you wins."

"Neither. Haven't you realized that we're average?"

"We all are. That's our fate."

"When a true genius appears, you can know him by the fact that all the dunces are in a confederacy against him."

"Jonathan Swift!"

"Bravo," says the lady. "You'll win. And then we'll celebrate. And then, perhaps, we'll get to know each other better."

"I'd really like that," says the young man next to her.

11.

Inheritance

David, who's occupying an aisle seat, looks about. "Where is she?"

"Who?" asks Marko, who's sitting by the window.

"Who, for God's sake. Surely not the Holy Ghost."

"He probably means the stewardess," offers Maya, who's sitting in the middle.

"I'd like something to drink."

"You have to wait," says Maya. "This isn't first class. When they come by with the cart and ask you what you want, then you order."

"That will be an hour."

"Here," Marko offers him a pocket-sized bottle of whiskey.

"How did you get that through security?"

"He shoved it in his underpants," says Maya and passes the bottle. "It looked like he had a hard on, and no one dared pat him down."

She twists off the cap and takes two long swigs.

"Hey," David grabs the bottle from her, "are you going to chug it all?"

"It's alright," says Marko, "I have another one." And he pulls another plastic bottle from his pocket.

"Sweet. And where did you hide that?"

"The same place as the other one," says Maya. "So it looked like he had a *really* big one. Who would dare pat him down? He could accuse them of sexual assault."

"Well, then I'll empty this one," says David and takes

a long swig.

"And I'll have a little of this," Maya reaches for the other bottle.

"No you won't," says Marko and shoves the bottle back in his pocket. "We're going to squat in these seats for twenty hours, can you believe it?"

"No, because we change planes in Singapore."

"Here or there, isn't it all the same?" yawns Maya.

"No, it isn't," says Marko. "You can't lie down here. You can't even spread your legs."

"Stop making fun of my broad," says David and sucks the last drop out of the bottle.

"Why shouldn't he," says Maya, "when everyone else does."

"Shut your trap!"

"Not so loud, David," Marko warns him. "People don't have to know what kind of lumpen they're sitting with."

"Let's try acting like we're respectable people."

"If you're good enough for foreign directors and an occasional ambassador, you belong to the respectable people. Doesn't matter what you do."

"It's about how we talk, not what we do, David," says Marko.

"That's right," Maya says. "Even a professional prostitute and her pimp have to act like a prince and princess."

"One more like that, and I'll smack you," David hisses in her ear.

"And how many people on this plane understand Slovene?"

"Almost everyone. Didn't you know that half the nation is moving to Australia?"

"By the way, how many times altogether have you flown?" Maya turns to him.

"Why do you want to know?"

"Just because."

"At least a hundred."

"I'd say never."

"Oh, yeah? And how can you tell, you super lucky hooker who would have to sell herself on the corner if it weren't for me."

"If you flew even once, you'd know that you shouldn't sneak whiskey through security. You can buy it in the duty free when you get inside."

"And what makes you think I didn't know that?"

"If you did, you wouldn't believe that your brother stuck the whiskey in his pants."

"And what makes you think I believed that?"

"Are you afraid of flying?"

"You ought to be more afraid of getting smacked than I should be of flying, and you're going to get it in a minute if you don't zip it."

"I'll yell, and they'll throw you off the plane."

"With a parachute?"

"When we land, the police will be waiting to arrest you for attacking a female passenger."

"When we land, I'll give you such a thumping that you won't go out for a week. Remember how it was last time?"

"No, dear David, your Maya doesn't forget a thing. She carefully files everything away, and when she's had her fill, she'll write an autobiography and take it directly to the police station."

"You forget I sold you to the police chief twice?"

"The reason I remember is that he got the smallest prick of all I have seen."

"They'll burn your autobiography, or better fuckography, on the spot. You're not safe anywhere. Except with me."

"David, please," Marko speaks up, nervously fidgeting. "Can we stop this?"

171

"Tell that to the woman sitting between us."

"I can't take this asinine bickering. Do it somewhere else, some other time. Not here, for God's sake."

"She always starts, I never do."

"Instead of being happy about everything we're looking forward to, and talking about that, you two keep on mocking each other."

"Tell her that."

"After all we're going to visit our father. Do you even remember him?"

"Who cares."

"He's our father."

"Really? He buried mom when you were twelve and I was four, packed us both off to an orphanage, and disappeared who knows where. And now he's our father?"

"Still you should be happy to finally see him. Now that you're grown up."

"Ha, ha," Maya laughs.

"Maya," Marko noticeably raises his voice, "now I'm also asking you to cut it out."

"I will," says Maya and slowly licks a finger. "I'm practicing for my next role. I'll probably get my first customer as soon as we land. I'm glad about it, I've never had an Australian."

"Maya…"

"Leave her alone, Marko, you can see she won't calm down. She's mad because she thinks she has a right to a part of the inheritance."

"I don't give a damn about the inheritance from your father. He probably doesn't even have anything. Except a kangaroo in the garden. He hasn't even died yet. Are you two planning to kill him?"

"You damn broad," David sighs. "What I'm going to do to you when we get to Sydney."

"You don't have to tell me," says Maya."

"The fact is our father's very sick," says Marko.

172

"Poor thing," David feigns sympathy. "He needs care, so he remembered his sons."

"And what was he doing all these years," Maya asks.

"He was living in America," says Marko. "He was an actor. Made quite a few action films. He sent me pictures."

"A film star!" Maya exclaims. "What does he look like?"

"How do you think my father looks," David sits up in his seat. Then he turns to Marko. "Does he look like me at all?"

"A lot."

"Well?" David turns to Maya.

"And now you like him all of a sudden?"

"No I don't. I'm just surprised he was an actor."

"He was already an actor when he left," says Marko. "You forget?"

"I was a kid, for God's sake, how am I supposed to know? But it would be different if he didn't leave. If he raised us like a father should, we wouldn't be what we are now."

"What are we?" Marko asks with surprise.

"Oh, for God's sake! Looks like you have a very high opinion of yourself."

"Funny words," Marko says with surprise. "Did you start reading books?"

"That'll be the day!" Maya chuckles.

"I'm not flying to Australia for someone there to make fun of me. I'll say hello. After all, he's my father. And then I'll leave."

"And if he's really sick?" Maya looks at him.

"Then it's our duty to take care of him?"

"The way I see it."

"On what planet did you pop out of the ground?"

"Judging by the pictures, I'd say he doesn't feel too good," Marko recalls, "and the pictures are a call for help. Why else would he send them?"

"What does he look like in them?" asks Maya.

"He has big bags under his eyes. And he's weirdly frightened. As if he felt death to be near."

"Those could be pictures of some of his roles," says Maya.

"I can't believe it," says David. "Our father writes to us after not even sending a postcard for a quarter century, and already it's smelling of incense and confession. He wants to see us to put some things in order, and we think he wants to write a will in our presence. Who's going to give us the money for the plane tickets when we find out none of this is true?"

"Me," says Maya. "From my work. As usual."

"You have to respect a nymphomaniac who others pay for her pleasures."

"A whore who's afraid that her pimp will kill her if she stops working for him deserves even more respect."

"We're back to that?" sighs Marko.

"You never know," says Maya, "maybe we'll be family in the end. Maybe your father will like me so much that he'll marry me and then die, and I'll inherit his fortune. And I'll keep you as my sons."

"It's also possible that I'll inherit the fortune and won't need you any more. And you'll have to find your own customers. It won't be nice."

"What's nice is the drink cart coming. I'm going to get so drunk that I'll vomit in your lap. That will be so pleasant. Unzip your zipper so I can vomit on your mini dick."

David gives her a slap.

12.

A Hollywood "Star's" Final Days

"Good afternoon. Pleased to meet you. Baumgartner is the name."

"O'Neil. Hello."

"What was wrong with the lady that demanded to be moved?"

"I have no idea. She said she's afraid of flying, and I tried to cure her."

"Right here, on the plane?"

"No one is afraid of flying when they're on the ground."

"And the lady didn't want your help?"

"Clearly not. Even though it's my profession. I'm a specialist in phobia therapy."

"Then today's my lucky day! I'm made of, put together from, and sewn out of phobias. You can imagine how they wrack my life."

"That's not apparent."

"Because I hide them."

"You manage well."

"I'm a professional actor. On disability for some time. Phobias made regular work impossible. And so now I'm playing my last role. Of a peaceful, well composed, late middle-aged gentleman who is put off by nothing."

"Then you are a really good actor."

"You know what they say. Once an actor, always an actor."

"What theater were you in?"

"Many. I also acted in quite a few films. I played Macbeth, Lear, Shylock, a traveling salesman, Tartuffe, and the male roles in almost all of Ibsen's plays. I played a murderer, detective, priest, and even a doctor. The list is almost longer than the list of phobias that plague me."

"Name them."

"You're not serious. We don't have enough time."

"You surely don't have them all. That would be abnormal."

"What's normal?"

"Most people are burdened by one, two, or three phobias. Ten at most. But not by all of them. After all, there're more than a hundred!"

"That's why I gave them all one name, so as not to get lost in the web. Like in a drama. There're lots of dialogues that are alike and at the same time different. But their common name is Hamlet."

"And the name of your phobias?"

"Anxiety."

"Anxiety isn't necessarily a phobia, unless it's extreme, then it is fear, or even terror."

"For me it's different degrees of anxiety. Feelings that are natural in their common form but too often explode into extremes."

"Give some examples."

"Whenever I'm afraid I sweat profusely. I get completely wet. And I have the feeling that my head is spinning and I'll faint."

"That's a standard symptom."

"Would you believe that at my wedding I almost ran from the altar?"

"A lot of people do that."

"But I was afraid everything would go wrong. That I'd look like a fool a hundred different ways. That I wouldn't survive the event."

"But you did."

"At my first child's birth, for which I wanted to be present only so as not to disappoint my wife, the delivery staff had more trouble with me that with her. I fainted twice in a row."

"Nothing unusual."

"But listen. I collapse so often it's almost impossible to believe, and always in the wrong place. Once in the middle of a performance I froze on stage and couldn't get a word out."

"That's awkward."

"I ran off stage more than once."

"That's even worse."

"Fear could seize me anywhere and without warning. On a train, on a bus, on a plane, walking down the street, or in the store. Even at home in bed I'm sometimes overwhelmed by a feeling that I'll die the next minute."

"Classic panic attack."

"But even when I don't have these attacks, I'm never calm. I'm worried something is wrong with my health, I'm worried about my financial status, or whether I'll even be able to survive. And about getting old and having to die. Can you imagine how I'm overcome by anxiety? It's enough for something to start knocking in my car, and I'm completely wet."

"And what are the symptoms of this anxiety?"

"It's like all my muscles and bones ache. I'm dizzy, my head hurts, I have goose bumps on my arms and legs, I feel like the flu is coming on. Sometimes it's hard to breathe or I can't swallow mucus."

"But these aren't classic phobias…"

"I haven't gotten to those. I'm afraid of open spaces and heights, that I'll faint, or get stuck in an elevator. I'm afraid of germs and cheese, I'm afraid of public speaking, flying, vomiting, and, of course, vomiting on an airplane."

"Those fears are called claustrophobia, agoraphobia, asthenophobia, bacillophobia, turophobia, sociophobia, aerophobia, emetophobia, and aeronausiphobia."

"I'm afraid I'm going to vomit." The man named Baumgartner pulls a sickness bag from the netting in front of him. "Sometimes, if I squeeze the paper bag in my hands long enough, it passes."

"Go on and squeeze it. How long have you had these fears?"

"Since I was little. They took me to a psychiatrist for the first time when I was ten."

"And?"

"It didn't help. Later in life I tried just about everything that's available: individual psychotherapy, group therapy, family therapy, cognitive therapy, rational-emotional therapy, hypnosis, meditation, self-help books, massage, prayer, acupuncture, yoga, Stoic philosophy, and then other such things I don't recall the names for."

"How about medicines? You never took any?"

"Medicines!" He frees the clasp on the pouch attached to his belt. "I have here thorazine, imipramine, desipramine, chlorpheniramine, Nardil, Prozac, Zoloft, Wellbutrin, Efexor, Levoxyl, propranolol, Serax, Centrax, Valium, Librium, Ativan, and Xanax."

"How often do you take them?"

"All the time. These ones, those ones. One every two hours. It's always different. That way I don't get hooked."

"And they help?"

"Depends when. There are times when I'm completely calm, but then I suddenly explode and am seized by fear that I'll do something terrible, kill, or shoot, or choke someone. Or hurt someone badly, which would be bad enough."

"But did that ever happen?"

"Not yet. Otherwise I probably wouldn't be sitting next to you. I'd be stuck in a psychiatric pen."

"Can I ask why you're flying to Australia?"

"I forget."

"You must be joking."

"No. The last two years I've been forgetting things. All at once, like a bolt from the blue, a cloud comes over me and completely shrouds my memory. So I don't know, this minute I don't know why I'm on this plane."

"And what will you do when we arrive?"

"I'll probably remember before then. It could be that someone will be waiting for me, someone I'll recognize. All in all I'm very worried, but that's part of the trouble I carry inside. But I've learned to count on nothing being as terrifying as it could be."

"For certain."

"Can you help me? You said you cure phobias."

"Forgetfulness is not a phobia."

"I know, but all the rest of it?

"It's difficult here, on a plane, in flight."

"Didn't you say you tried to cure the lady who then demanded to be moved?"

"Fear of flying is another thing…"

"No, no. Fear of flying is a phobia, and you said that you specialize in curing phobias. Why her and not me? What's wrong with me?"

"I'm sorry but I have to ask you to allow me to pass. I have to go to the restroom."

"Right now?"

"It's urgent."

"I'm not accustomed to accommodating everyone to whom something comes to mind, but here you go."

He gets up and allows his neighbor to squeeze past him. Then he moves to the seat by the window.

The therapist hurries to the restroom, but doesn't go in. Instead, he looks for a stewardess.

"Is something wrong, sir? You're rather pale."

"Please change my seat. Anywhere. The gentleman next to me is completely… very… he shouldn't be on a plane at all."

"Unfortunately I can't keep moving passengers."

"Please."

"Before it was the lady next to you that demanded to be moved, and now you. Is something wrong with the seat?"

"No, the seat is fine, but… Let the lady return, and let the gentleman go back to his seat."

"Sir, this is highly unusual…"

"Please. I beg you."

"And if she doesn't want to?"

"Then I'll lock myself in one of the restrooms and stay there until we land. It may be that I'll be injured or even asphyxiated."

"My God, what a day," sighs the stewardess and sets off towards the lady in the blue jacket, her eyes closed and hands folded, who is mumbling something that could well be a prayer.

***

The stewardess returns to the phobia doctor, who in the meantime took the seat on which the man named Baumgartner had been sitting. The latter now sits by the window.

"Unfortunately it won't work, sir. No one wants to change seats."

"That's alright. I'll bear it."

"I'm glad."

"I'll get a hold of myself, as they say."

"The gentleman won't disturb you anymore, isn't that right?" the stewardess looks at the actor.

"Disturb? Me?" he turns to the doctor. "I was disturbing you?"

"Not at all. It's a mistake."

"Then everything's fine," says the stewardess.

"Bring each of us a double whiskey, and it will be," says the doctor and turns to the actor. "You'll have one, right?"

"With pleasure, misunderstandings have to be patched up, the flight is long."

"I'll bring them," says the stewardess and goes off.

"I had a mad fear," says the doctor. "It happens to me, too, once in a while."

"To be honest, most of my phobias come from a big mistake that I made in my life."

"Better to talk about something else?"

"But I need advice. It's such an unusual thing that it ought to interest you."

The doctor sighs. "If there's no other way."

"The mistake I regret to this day is sending my two boys to an orphanage and disappearing."

"Small children?"

"One was twelve, the other four."

"Why did you do that?"

"My wife had died, and I saw my sons as stumbling blocks to my goal."

"Which was?"

"To become a recognized and successful actor."

"And ever since then you've regretted that inhuman act."

"It seems inhuman to you?"

"I know you're not the only one in the world to have done something like that, but I can't praise you for such an act."

"I don't expect that. I'd only like you to hear my story and give me advice."

"I'm afraid I'm not the right audience. I cure phobias."

"It's one of my phobias. The worst."

"I don't understand."

"The fear that my sons won't give me a chance to correct my mistake."

"But do you know where they are and what they're

doing?"

"A while ago I hired a detective, who found them and learned the details of their lives."

"No doubt they're exceptionally successful. That's typical of children who grow up in orphanages."

"That's not the way it is with them."

"But all the same they have normal lives."

"I can't say that. The younger one makes a living pimping, selling his wife to politicians, bankers, businessmen, and rich foreigners. Since she's exceptionally beautiful, he makes more off her that I did in my best acting years."

"Nice."

"According to the information I received from the detective, the girl doesn't dare run away, because my son threatens to kill her."

"What about the older one?"

"He's a little more normal. He sells drugs, not women. After he served three years in prison, he became more cautious. I'm afraid he's gay."

"That's probably the least of your worries."

"The sons I abandoned out of naked egotism when they needed me most have become images of my detestable act."

"Doesn't it seem a little late for regrets?"

"And nothing came of my career either. It's true I got parts, even some in Hollywood, and earned relatively handsome sums, but I played Hamlet, Lear, Helmer, and other great characters for the most part on amateur stage. I wanted to prove that I *am* an actor."

"But if you got parts in Hollywood…"

"My longest film part lasted three minutes. I had to beat a policeman. And then another one. I was supposed to be very good at such things. I was a hotel doorman, a taxi driver, a vegetable store manager, a prisoner, a crowd member, and so on. In short, I got parts that anyone else could have played, maybe even better."

"I can believe that that doesn't generate pleasant feelings."

"I'm a loser. A total loser. And I dreamt of becoming a legend, a star, recipient of five Oscars."

"Few people don't overestimate their abilities at critical moments."

"Small comfort."

"And you sons? Did you make contact with them during this time?"

"By mail. I would send the older one pictures of my roles. In the sick hope that they would be proud of their father's successes."

"Did they ever reply?"

"Never. I didn't give a return address."

"Would you even recognize them if you met them? They're men now, not boys."

"No. And they'd be even less likely to recognize me. In the pictures I sent to the oldest, I was always in some role and accordingly made up. If I appeared before them now, they wouldn't have a clue who I am."

"A sad story."

"Now you understand why a hundred phobias are destroying me?"

"Evidently your feeling of guilt manifested itself psychosomatically. And profusely. In all my years of practice, I've never encountered such a radical case."

"I know you can't cure me. It's simply impossible. It's enough that you listen to me."

"A book should be written about you."

"Better not. No one should find out how low a person can fall."

"A person who his whole life shamelessly and without regret put himself first."

"But..."

"But?"

"I invited my sons to Sydney, where I'm living."

"I won't ask how you got to Sydney from Hollywood, but it's nice of you to invite them. Why?"

"I'd like to get to know them. And I'd like them to get to know me."

"Did they answer?"

"Yes. They're coming."

"I'm surprised."

"I mentioned in passing the possibility of an estate, an inheritance, and the like."

"Then they're coming for money."

"I hope because of me, too. Because it's time we knew each other."

"Are you rich?"

"A one bedroom apartment in a building overlooking the opera. 15,000 Australian dollars on my account."

"That's all you have to leave them?"

"I know they expect more. But it's more important that we get acquainted and forgive each other."

"What do you have to forgive them?"

"They could have made an effort to find me."

"Are all actors the same?"

"I don't understand."

"That you exist only for yourselves, and all others are just an audience?"

"I hope not."

"And when will your sons come for this inheritance?"

"I have to die before they can get it. That will be soon, because I'm sick. But they're supposed to come any time. That's why I flew to London, so that we could meet there first, on neutral territory, and work out our problems before going to Sydney together."

"And?"

"Unfortunately the detective I hired botched it. He told me that they were leaving yesterday, today, or tomorrow. But he couldn't say with which airline."

"So it's theoretically possible that they're sitting on this plane."

"Theoretically. But that would be too great a coincidence."

"I've heard a lot of stories, but never such a cruel one. I'm filled with a desire to choke you to death right here, on this plane."

"But you cure people…"

"Of different illness than you have. It would be better that you had never been born."

"Can you help me?"

"The feeling of guilt is the best medicine."

"But it hurts. Is pain all that's left in the end?"

"Unfortunately. Unless you have a heart attack while having an orgasm."

13.

In vino veritas

"Look, I know this is something new to you, but you're a little too worried."
"Easy for you. You're like a fish in water in Australia."
"The business is registered. The agreements with suppliers are signed. We even have a secretary in Sydney. All we need is five or six employees."
"I invested everything that was left after bankruptcy."
"Are we friends or not?"
"I'm going into an unfamiliar business environment."
"Business is business whether you're in Botswana, Australia, or Slovenia."
"Isn't selling Slovene wine in Australia, which is one of the biggest wine exporters, rather risky?"
"Name one business venture that isn't."
"Yes, I know…"
"Haven't we discussed it all a hundred times?"
"Yes."
"I didn't hide anything from you. I can assure you that our biggest problem will be how to deposit the profits in a tax haven."
"I have some experience with that."
"We'll need a team for successful advertising, to sell to hoteliers, and for deliveries. Administrative personnel. How will we find people who won't cheat us?"
"It will be hard to avoid that."
"You mean to say that employees in Australia cheat

like at home?"

"There's no country on earth where that doesn't happen."

"You mean to say we'll be victims of cheats no matter who we hire?"

"To what extent depends on us."

"What about good old honesty, loyalty to your employer, and mutual trust?"

"Did you get stuck in a time that no longer exists?"

"What can we do to avoid jail?"

"We have to be careful."

"And what does that mean?"

"A CEO allocates a hundred million from public funds to a consulting agency his wife owns, without there ever being any consulting. A cashier in a supermarket intentionally forgets to scan an item worth two dollars, because she wants to help a poor neighbor. Who is the bigger thief?"

"They're both at fault."

"And the two of us, who are going to avoid taxes by paying most of our profits to a fraudulent consulting agency in the Cayman Islands?"

"That's something else. The state literally robs businessmen, who constantly risk going bankrupt. Keeping some money out of their clutches is almost a duty. We're the ones taking a risk. Why should the state live off us? To some extent it can, but taxmen are so voracious that they rob you of the desire to work."

"I see you have these things figured out."

"I'd like to know how we can avoid our employees' cheating."

"Only by allowing a *little* cheating."

"Are you joking?"

"Almost everyone cheats or steals at work. According to some surveys, ninety percent of people are even prepared to admit it."

"What kind of things should we allow?"

"It's hard to decide in advance, because we don't know how they'll try to swindle us. We'll keep an eye on things and decide as we go."

"That will be a challenge."

"Not at all. In Australia, cheats at work are divided into wolves, hawks, and donkeys."

"What does that mean?

"The wolves are, for example, railroad workers, because they always steal in packs. Last year a train derailed, because the engineer fell asleep. That shouldn't have happened, because according to the rules a second engineer should have been there. But he wasn't."

"Was he sick?"

"No. Officially he was on the train, because at the shift change he came to the station and reported for work. They found him at home in bed after the accident."

"Was he fired?"

"Don't be silly. It's completely normal for a second engineer to report for work and then go home, or to his lover, or a nightclub. Or even to another job. The system is such that it permits this. Even second engineers who don't want to cheat work only a half hour a day. That's the agreement between engineers and their bosses."

"So why are railroad workers wolves?"

"They can't cheat except in packs, by agreement between the engineers, station officials, and inspectors. They cover each others' asses."

"But that's not possible in all lines of work."

"And how! The worst wolves are refuse collectors, who collect and haul away garbage in packs. They cheat in all kinds of ways. Their first rule of employment says they can't accept tips. The second is that everything they collect is the company's property. But!"

"But?"

"If someone asks them to take things away that by

the rules they're not supposed to touch—for example, furniture, mattresses, refrigerators, and all the things the garbage truck's compactor can't crush—they bargain on a price."

"Off the books."

"Of course. The head of the crew, the foreman, can always bargain. The wolves have a strict hierarchy and loyalty—one for all and all for one. Whether it comes from tips or extra items, the money has to go into the kitty. Whatever is collected, the members of the group divide up after work."

"Some honesty amidst dishonesty."

"Every member of the group, which usually has five collectors, has five baskets fixed to the truck. One is for bronze, another for iron, a third for copper, a fourth for glass, and a fifth for bricks. People throw out all kinds of things, even clothing and broken bicycle parts. That's how the refuse collectors increase their income by thirty percent."

"At least you have to give them credit for being resourceful."

"Even more so than businessmen."

"What about the hawks?"

"Those are people who can't stand work rules and responsibilities and determine the nature, conditions, and amount of work themselves. They are store and small business owners, industrial and commercial sales reps, professors, journalists, dentists, lawyers, and independent taxi drivers. Being self-employed, they have benefits that others can only dream of."

"And us two? Will we be big or small business owners?"

"That depends on which type will most benefit us."

"What's the difference?"

"If we're small, we'll have to cover all personnel expenses ourselves. That's the fastest way to bankruptcy. If we're a big business, we can hire subcontractors, who will pay health and social security contributions themselves, but they'll have more opportunities to hide and cover things up. That, of course, will be their problem, not ours."

"Hide what?"

"Not so much hide as withhold things from us. Mostly put in expenditures. They charge for travel they didn't do. And per diems. A friend sends you a bill for staying in his hotel. Who can prove you weren't there? We can make things easier, for example, by not even booking the delivery of certain wines."

"I don't know if I'd be happy with that."

"Haven't you done business in Slovenia?"

"I don't know the rules in Australia and don't want to land up in jail."

"Our secretary will teach you all about it. I made you two a reservation for a week's vacation on Stradbroke Island, off Brisbane. Endless sand beaches, privacy... You'll be eternally grateful."

"Wait a minute, how old is she?"

"Twenty-three."

"And she already knows about these things?"

"She studied management."

"Don't forget I have a wife and two children in Slovenia."

"Did I say you have to give them up? We going to be importing and selling wine, but that doesn't mean we have to be drunk the whole time. But you can enjoy a little drunkenness in small doses."

"With the secretary on a sandy beach."

"No one is forcing you."

"How did you put it? Wolves, hawks, and donkeys."

"We belong to the hawks, and our secretary to the donkeys. Her family is Malaysian. Her name is Guat."

"And even though she's Malaysian..."

"...she's familiar with the mysteries of Australian business. She was born in Australia. You'll have to get used to the fact that Australia is a multi-racial country. Almost everyone's ancestors were born somewhere else."

"And this—Guat you said—is one of the donkeys?"

"By occupation she should be, but she's too smart. A typical example of a donkey is a supermarket cashier, who sits at the register all day and takes in money for purchases. At first glance, she doesn't have much opportunity to cheat. The danger of the manager catching her or a customer complaining is too great. That's why she doesn't cheat customers but her employer. She rings up less than the purchases are worth and pockets the difference."

"In Slovenia that's no longer possible."

"That's why we located the business in Australia. Would you like to keep filling bank holes on the sunny side of the Alps?"

"I know, but…"

"She rings up only a third of value of goods her mother, father, brother, uncle, aunt, brother-in-law, cousin, girlfriend, boyfriend, or husband comes to buy. If you consider that an average size supermarket employs from six to eight cashiers, and each one has at least ten relatives and friends, that's eighty people who can carry away three times more than they paid for every week."

"You want to tell me we live in a world where everyone cheats, each according to available opportunities?"

"What kind of a world did you think we live in?"

"It's pretty depressing, don't you think?"

"Are you going to tell me, halfway to Australia, that I have picked the wrong partner?"

"I'm talking about my feelings. And they're not pleasant."

"If only we were cheating, mine wouldn't be either. Fortunately, one way or another, the whole world is cheating. Even the Church. Everyone lies, everyone pretends. By the way, how much money do you still have in tax havens?"

"I put everything into our venture. To the last cent."

"Then why aren't you looking forward to the results?"

"I don't usually have that problem. Only when I'm on a plane. That can crash at any moment. Then I have great regret for everything I've done wrong in my life."

"What did you do wrong? You're a trader. You're subject to the laws of the free market!"

"All the same. The world is different than I imagined when I was young."

"It became different."

"Unfortunately."

"It's a matter of survival. It's the only game we have left. I hope you don't leave me in the lurch."

"You know very well I won't."

***

"There will be many competitors. We mustn't forget that. Do you know who all is selling wine on the Australian market?"

"French, Italians, Spanish, Argentines, Californians, South Africans, and even Croatians and Serbs. The whole world. What chance do we have with our Karst concoctions?"

"I can remember the time when I was living in London as a student. The best selling wine in Britain then was Laško Riesling. Two million bottles a year were imported."

"Because it was cheap."

"Because it was cheap and good. And because importers knew how to fool the competition."

"Fool? Is that what we have to do?"

"You know full well that this work is war. We'll need a strategy. We'll have to adapt the strategy along the way. It will be stressful but fun."

"Until now, I've put all my knowledge and energy into production, never sales. So understand me if I confess to having mixed feelings. Sales demand different abilities, ones I might not have."

"I'll teach you everything I know."

"And if I can't take it in?"

"Don't be silly. The main thing is to know how to judge people, to see through them, and immediately notice if they're trying to cover something up. Here I mostly have in mind people we'll have to hire as traveling salesmen."

"And where are we going to find them?"

"It might sound funny, but I trust Slovenes most of all. With them it's easy to tell if they're hiding something. And there's more than enough of them in Australia."

"But not all of them are necessarily fit to sell wine."

"That's true, but this pessimism of yours won't help us. We'll find a way. I'm telling you we'll find the best ones. And then the whole thing will only be a matter of strategy."

"Can you tell me a little more about that?"

"Look, people are selfish by nature. Aren't we? Always and everywhere our thinking revolves foremost around our interests. We ask ourselves how something will impact us. How will it help us? But at the same time—and this is normal—we try to hide our selfishness, mask it, and make it look like loyalty and concern for others. That will be our biggest problem as directors."

"And what will we do?"

"Everything will seem fine at first. Everyone will be enthusiastic, trustworthy, and anxious to make a good impression. Then we'll start to notice that this or that person has started to use his position and our trust to further his interests. If we don't clamp down in time, one morning we'll realize that we're employing a bunch of selfish, deceitful individuals."

"And then?"

"Then we'll have to avoid the most common

mistakes that managers make at that point. The majority say to themselves: we have to improve work morale, motivate the workers, and award them for good work once in a while. And they very soon realize that they've spoiled their employees and even reinforced their selfishness. An even worse mistake is to try and punish them, to enforce discipline, which arouses resentment in people and makes them defensive."

"If those are all mistakes, what then?"

"They're mistakes because poor managers engage in problem solving too late. It's a waste of time to think about emphasizing work morale when it's already gone. It has to be emphasized from the very start."

"How?"

"You have to take an example from military leaders who made history. They know how to turn selfish individuals into a group that believed it was fighting for the same, worthy goal. Every person has inside a desire to be part of something greater. The more important the group goal, the less time there is to devote to thinking about personal interests. They'll start equating their success with the group's success. They'll begin to comprehend that selfish acts will shame them in the eyes of the others."

"That sounds nice. My managers obviously did not possess that knowledge, otherwise the business wouldn't have failed."

"You're starting to understand. The workers have to be united in battle for a goal that means something to all of them. They have to be convinced that they are fighting for an idea."

"Even though this is about selling wine?"

"Or tires. Or lighters. Or disposable razors. You yourself know that you have only three options in the market: you win, you stagnate, or you lose. I'm offering you the option of winning together."

"I'm not saying I'm ungrateful to you for the

opportunity, but once you fail, you become cautious."

"Caution is always in order, but you've become rigid."

"It will be fine, I'll lose my doubts once things come together. When I see we've hired the right people. When I see that there's interest in Slovene wines."

"There's always interest in good wines for the right price."

"What did you sell before you got into wines?"

"I told you. Real estate. But there's a crisis in Australia. Prices are sky high, sales have slowed, before long the balloon will burst, and prices will be halved. I got out at the right time. What did you do before you started the factory swim floats that went under?"

"I sold swim floats imported from China. Then I said to myself, why don't I make them? And I did. Then the Chinese cut their prices and I went under, even though mine were better."

"I studied management. Well, I didn't exactly study. I took three courses, but that was enough."

"Education is of no use without talent."

"And now you're going to give me worries in addition to those I already have?"

"One more glass and I'll be fine."

"Aren't you almost drunk?"

"Not at all. You have no idea how much I can take."

"I know your habit. That's why I insisted we travel economy. Upstairs you're entitled to as much alcohol as you can hold. Here there's a limit. Perhaps they'll decide that you've exceeded yours. But no matter. I'm going to the restroom. On the way I'll ask the stewardess to bring us two more whiskies. After all, we're on Singapore Airlines.

He gets up and heads to the restroom, which is quite far away. After some time the stewardess brings two glasses of whiskey and ice. The director of the factory that made swim floats empties the first one and then the second. Then he asks a stewardess who happens to pass by to take away both glasses.

His companion returns ten minutes later.

"Well, would you believe it!" he says when he has squeezed his body into the seat.

"Long line?" asks his business partner.

"We've informally hired the first three employees for Slovenian Wines Australia."

"Right on the plane?"

"On the way back I heard a line of Slovene nearby: Wine is the only drink for people who think they're better than others. And it hit me: that could be our company slogan! Can you imagine? Advance acknowledgment to potential buyers that they're not part of the crowd."

"Exclusivity?"

"Why not?"

"Not something that would attract the crowd?"

"There is no more crowd. It's broken up into segments that want to differ based on what they like. The consumer wants to be part of a group that can give the impression of being something special."

"And who said that?"

"There are three of them, two young men and a girl sitting between them. I don't know which of the young men said it, but I turned around after a few steps and spoke to them."

"And hired them?"

"Judging by the way they talk, they're not that educated. One even swears a little too much, but that's not a problem. They seem to me intelligent, sharp, and experienced. People who understand that the first duty in life is to survive."

"But is that enough to work for us?"

"Look, we'll need a warehouse person. The girl can do odd jobs in the office. The one who swears says that he's expecting a substantial inheritance, although it's not for sure, but I quickly convinced him that it's good to have a job, at least temporarily, in order to get a residence permit."

"Even though you don't know them."

"Intuition, my partner, intuition. I know how to analyze a person's character. I gave them my address and invited them to stop by, because we will need workers as soon as we arrive. We'll see later. If they work out, fine. If not, we'll fire them."

"Who would have thought that you can get a job in Australia on a flight to Sydney?"

"I'm pretty proud that I did that for someone."

"Do they speak English?"

"I forgot to ask. But they must, otherwise why would they be going to Australia for an inheritance?"

"And loyalty to the group you were talking about? Are they capable of that? Or are we hiring three selfish people we know nothing about?"

"I'm never mistaken about that. What about that whiskey? Haven't they brought it?"

"Not yet." He gets up. "I'm going to the restroom. I'll order again on the way."

"A double. We deserve it, seeing how we hired our first three workers."

"Where are these three sitting?"

"Leave them alone. You'll only confuse them. They might change their minds."

"They won't if they're serious."

"Look. Are we partners? I like the girl. She's a little dim, tired, as if something's bothering her, but she's sexy. Crazy sexy. You'll go on vacation with our Malaysian secretary. I can't live without a bit on the side. Just as you can't do without whiskey."

"I hope you know what you're doing."

"Always, my friend, always."

14.

A Bomb on Board

"And so you say you're going back to Australia?"

"I've had enough of England. And the English, too, to be honest. Of their customs."

"Which ones?"

"The English can be utterly obnoxious."

"Can you be more precise?"

"As an Irishman, you ought to know English customs."

"You can tell my Irish accent?"

"Does that bother you?"

"No, I'm proud of it. You know us after all—the Irish, how patriotic we are."

"And how. I was married to an Irish woman."

"Fascinating! And where is she now?"

"She returned home out of patriotism. To some village on the west coast."

"And you're going to Australia. Out of patriotism."

"It's hard for Australia to become a person's home. Especially if you weren't born there. I'm returning because I can't stand Englishmen."

"Why can't you stand them?"

"Besides, you Irish aren't at all patriotic. There're several million living around the world. Can you say how many of them have returned home?"

"Your wife, for example?"

"Your cynicism causes me to think you're probably not Irish but English."

"In short, what you don't like about the English is their cynicism."

"If that were all, I'd gladly await my death in London."

"Yet the English are the most polite people in the world."

"Especially the soccer fans, who bust up at least half the town wherever they go."

"According to that logic, you could designate half of Ireland terrorists."

"Why?"

"On account of the bombs that the IRA used to throw at British soldiers and civilians."

"That was a freedom struggle, not frenzied brawling by hooligans."

"There're hooligans everywhere; it's not an English peculiarity."

"It's a matter of upbringing, from the cradle on. That's what makes an Englishman an Englishman."

"And a hooligan?"

"Did you know that almost all British prime ministers have been orphans or illegitimate? And on account of their lacking parents in early childhood, they spent their adult years as victims of personality disorders?"

"Almost all?"

"A third."

"But British prime ministers were not even all English."

"Well, some indeed were not."

"At least seven were Scots, two Irishmen, and two Welsh. One was even born in Canada."

"You sound more English than Irish."

"I'm not defending the English, I'm defending the facts."

"They may in fact have been born elsewhere, but the English raised and educated them."

"That's possible, but you still haven't told me which English customs caused you to return to Australia."

"Every year a quarter million British disappear! Can you imagine? And they only find fifty thousand of them."

"You think they disappear because they're tired of English customs?"

"Only God can answer that question."

"God himself is English, as a sixteenth-century bishop of London said."

"A classic example of English logic. If God is an Englishman, there are no English, because not all the English can be gods, and God cannot be simply one of them."

"Shall we order another glass of red wine?"

"Let's. I'll go ahead and push the button."

"So it's their customs that you can't take anymore."

"Let's talk about that later. First I'd like to lay out some more facts that will surprise you. For example..."

"For example?"

"How many vacant houses do you think there are in Britain?"

"Would I be mistaken if I said quite a few?"

"767,000."

"But that's almost a million!"

"And in London alone there are 128,000! And how many people in Britain are officially homeless?"

"Tell me."

"380,000! And how much does homelessness cost the British taxpayer? One billion, four hundred million pounds a year. Doesn't it seem to you that something is wrong here?"

"Absolutely. Lack of political will?"

"English indifference, which suffuses every layer of society."

"Has the society really changed that much?"

"Perhaps I'm exaggerating."

"Indeed."

"What I want to say is that among the British I

perceive the English most negatively. I have plenty of cause to disparage the Irish in view of the fact that my wife fled our wedding bed in the middle of the night and returned to Ireland. All she wrote on the message she left me was, 'I don't love you. I love Jesus.'"

"A religious nut."

"No. It turned out that Jesus was a Spaniard named Jesus Madrigal Agosta, and not even a real Spaniard, but a black man from Venezuela who was trying to use her to get a residence permit in a European Union country."

"Yes, things always come out for what they are in the end."

"Don't get the idea that I'm returning to Australia because of that."

"I know, you're returning on account of English customs."

"I'm returning because every year two thousand British die from pain killers, which they can get without a prescription."

"Aspirin, acetaminophen, things like that?"

"And many more."

"That's why you're returning? People in Australia take aspirin for pain as well."

"But not every day and not regularly for years."

"Are you sure?"

"Do you know what the third leading cause of death is in Britain?"

"Traffic accidents?"

"Visits to the doctor."

"Don't tell me they kill patients?"

"Deaths caused by medical error following a heart attack or cancer is the most common cause of death in America."

"But that doesn't hold for Britain."

"Things are even worse there."

"But that can't go for the English, whom you claim

you can't stand."

"Did I say that?"

"That's how our conversation started."

"In Britain, eight patients *a day* die on account of medical errors. Three thousand a year."

"Those are frightening statistics, but…"

"We live in an extremely dangerous world. The ones who are supposed to save our lives are killing us."

"Are you a doctor?"

"Where did you get that idea?"

"I have the feeling that only a doctor can have so much information about these things. Perhaps in England you committed an error that resulted in a patient's death, but they let you off. And you're returning to Australia to continuing practicing as far as possible from the scene of the crime."

"You know…"

"Not really crime, but as far as possible from where things came apart."

"I'm not a doctor. I'm a patient who one of those English doctors almost killed. Psychologically, it's true, but that's the worst. I'm returning to Australia in the hope of finding someone who can cure me."

"May I ask of what illness?"

"And you admit that you're not Irish but English."

"How did you guess?"

"I'm a professor of diction at the Royal Academy of Dramatic Art in London. I don't miss any accent. I'd even bet that you were born in Yorkshire."

"Bravo. Then we can continue where we started, disparaging the English."

"Now it will be more difficult. And what is your occupation, if I may ask?"

"I'm a doctor. If you share the details of your illness with me, I might be able to help."

"No, I'd rather wait for the wine we ordered."

***

"So? On account of what illness are you returning to Australia?"

"As a doctor, you're of course interested."

"Doctors are continually educating ourselves."

"If that were only so!"

"Some of us."

"You've certainly heard of my illness. It's call the world"

"You mean…?"

"That's it. The world hurts. It hurts so much that I feel it in every fiber of my body, in every nerve and every nerve cell."

"So it has to do with the world, not the English?"

"Doesn't the world seem fatally ill?"

"No doubt not everything is as it should be…"

"But?"

"The end isn't as near as some say. It can still be saved."

"How?"

"We have to make an effort."

"Come on now. You're making an effort for every fifth person on Earth not to have to live on less than a dollar a day?"

"I myself can do very little in that regard."

"So let everyone else make an effort."

"We all have to. All of us together. Everyone in the world."

"Come on."

"I know it's complicated, but the main thing is that we don't despair."

"Which is to say we can't do anything, but we can hope that things will take care of themselves."

"I didn't say that…"

"Like most people, you don't see any farther than the end your nose."

"Now…"

"The world doesn't hurt, because you're not interested in it. And since you're not interested, you don't know what state it is in."

"You can't fault me for that."

"Your interest in the world goes no farther than the morning paper, which you scan before going to work. Perhaps something inside worries you, even terrifies you, but that's where it stops. Then you keep on living as if the world were just fine."

"This is going nowhere…"

"Do you know that a third of the world is involved in wars?"

"Of course I know."

"Do you know that a fifth of mankind goes to bed without having eaten even a crust of bread? Does that seem right to you?"

"Far from it…"

"Do you know that every year more people commit suicide than die in all wars put together?"

"I didn't know that, but it could be true."

"Do you know that ten languages die every year? That in 150 countries—that is, the vast majority—the law permits torture? That climate change is already killing over one hundred fifty thousand people a year?"

"I don't know the details, but don't doubt that you're right."

"Do you know that three hundred thousand children are fighting in armed conflicts on different continents? And forty-five million Indian children are forced to work for a handful of rice a day? And that even today thirty million people are in slavery?"

"I agree that those are catastrophic figures…"

"But if we all make an effort, the problems will be

solved?"

"Look, I didn't mean..."

"It's possible you're right. Every hour—note, every hour—Americans throw out two and a half million plastic bottles. Every three weeks there are enough of them that, tied together, they would make a ladder long enough to climb to the Moon."

"I can no longer tell whether you're joking or whether your cynicism is part of the illness you say you have."

"Do you know that every day people worldwide buy a million cell phones?"

"But that's good."

"Increasing drivel about nothing?"

"Imagine you live in an isolated village somewhere on the edge of the Sahara. And your father has a heart attack. If you have a cell phone, you can do what you otherwise couldn't. You call for help."

"And how will help get to your father? On a camel? Ten days after he's buried?"

"I said that things are complicated..."

"So we throw up our hands? And stick with what we've attained, as if it isn't possible for us to lose everything tomorrow?"

"I'm aware of that, and others are, too."

"And despite that no one does anything."

"Look, I'm a doctor. I save lives and ease people's pain. Even here, on this flight, I had to inject an eight-year old boy with a sedative when he was having an attack of hysteria."

"But you can't cure the illness of the world that I have."

"Don't be offended, but it seems to me that in your case it's a specific form of depression."

"Before you accused me of joking, and now you're the one joking."

"We can go on all the way to Sydney about how the world is sick. But we won't solve anything. The only thing we can change is the way we feel."

"With pills?"

"Sure, if it turns out they help."

"The world is going to ruin, it's not a good feeling, take an aspirin?"

"The pain is not in the world itself, the pain is in our attitude."

"Meaning, I have to change my attitude."

"That's right."

"I have to learn to close my eyes, lie to myself and others, and convince myself that while things are terrible, I can do absolutely nothing, and so am guilty of nothing. It's possible the world has been *condemned* to destruction and I'm just one of the victims?"

"For how long have you been experiencing the world as an illness?"

"Long enough that the time isn't far off when it will send me to my grave."

"Did the illness get worse after your wife left you?"

"Don't be offended, but such questions don't befit someone who claims to be a doctor."

"Why? People often fall ill when something like that happens. They feel betrayed, humiliated, worthless…"

"And they start blaming their wife, who found a better partner in another man, for everything that's wrong with the world?"

"When a man loses the most precious person in his life, he often changes completely and becomes cruel, vengeful…"

"Exactly. I want vengeance. For everything that went wrong in the world."

"On your wife?"

"Oh for God's sake. I wish her five orgasms a day. Until she's so worn out that she begs me on her knees to take her back."

"Would you?"

"Yes. Only in order to abandon her in a month."

"Which means you're no better than her."

"Compared with the vengeance I'm planning, that would be a nick in the wall."

"What are you planning?"

"Vengeance on everyone who made the world an illness for me."

"On the English?"

"Why?"

"On the Americans?"

"Best on both, but why?"

"Aren't they most to blame for the world being the way it is?"

"Do you think it's on the edge of disaster?"

"Let's say."

"And you, an Englishman, are saying that?"

"I was born in England, but my ancestors were Jews from Ukraine."

"My ancestors were probably Huns, who after the death of their chief Attila, remained in the Roman Empire. There were almost a million of them. Do you think they stopped reproducing?"

"Highly unlikely."

"Then there's a piece of Hun in all of us. And when it takes charge, we decide on vengeance."

"Which we can also reject, being not only Huns, but also Romans, Germans, Slavs, Jews, and whatever else."

"Exactly. Considering that Germans and Slavs are known for being able to reject vengeance."

"I suggest we put aside these depressing problems and continue offending the English. That's how we began. And it was fun."

"You're not interested in what vengeance I'm planning?"

"Not at all. Most of all because I see no one you could take vengeance on."

"You don't?"

"You can't take it on everyone who has driven the world to the edge of destruction."

"How about a smaller group of people I identify as accomplices? For example, the ones on this plane?"

"Wait…"

"Is it starting to penetrate your brain?"

"You're not thinking…"

"Could be."

"I think this joke has gone too far."

"What if it's not a joke?"

"As a doctor who also studied psychology, I think it's hard to categorize you as a person who would believe that he can save the world by sacrificing 500 innocent lives."

"Vengeance has nothing to do with common sense."

"I suggest we stop the tasteless jokes and go back to offending the English, Irish, Americans, Jews, Russians, Chinese, and all peoples living below the clouds."

"You won't turn me in?"

"To whom, why?"

"To the captain. The staff. The air marshal."

"What would I tell them?"

"That there's a terrorist sitting next to you who is going to detonate a bomb over the Bay of Bengal."

"Don't be offended, but our conversation has started to weary me. Perhaps you've enjoyed too much wine. If you don't mind, I'll nap for half an hour."

"In half an hour you'll be awakened by a terrible explosion that will end your pleasant dreams forever."

"That's alright. Eternity awaits all of us in the future, so why not sooner rather than later?"

He makes himself comfortable in his seat and closes his eyes.

"I hope you're not sorry."

"As a doctor, I'm only sorry when I can't cure a patient."

"I'm the world. And the world is incurably ill. Isn't suicide the only honorable solution?"

"Ask the stewardess to bring you another glass of wine."

***

"Is that the end of our conversation or shall we continue?"

"Would you like to?"

"I'm in the mood."

"But not about a bomb onboard."

"We could continue disparaging the English."

"Would you find that fun?"

"A great deal."

"Even though we'd be disparaging me, too, since I'm English."

"You said you're a descendant of Ukrainian Jews."

"Then the descendants of William the Conqueror aren't English?"

"Sure, after a thousand years. But you said your parents…"

"Grandparents. My parents were born in England. Do I, too, need a thousand years to become an Englishman?"

"I have to confess that my wife wasn't Irish. She was English."

"I guessed that."

"But if you see yourself as English, you won't want to play along with disparaging, as I'm suggesting."

"On the contrary. We English enjoy making fun of ourselves."

"I hadn't noticed."

"I'm surprised."

"Have you heard the German saying that Germans

invent things, the French copy them, and the English make good money selling them?"

"The English think it a crime anything the lower classes do that the upper classes find tasteless."

"And they talk as if they had a handful of plums in their mouths, and then, after having swallowed them, they're left with a blockage in their throats from the pits."

"Only true Englishmen."

"Not many of those around. You need a magnifying glass to find them in London."

"Shall we also disparage the Irish, Poles, Italians, Pakistanis, Indians, islanders from the Caribbean, blacks, and Chinese—-that is, most of London's residents?"

"Only the English."

"Then we can't skip Goethe, who said he heard of an Englishman who hung himself to be free of the daily stress of dressing and undressing."

"As long as we're on the Germans, let's not forget what people in the former East Germany dared to say publicly about the English."

"I don't know about that."

"Paralytic ass lickers, effeminate traitors to mankind, servile imitators, arch cowards and collaborators, a gang of women killers, parasitic traditionalists, playboy soldiers, and fanciful dandies in a degenerate's paradise."

"Excellent. What about the German saying that there're two priests in a group of three Italians, two braggarts in a group of three Spaniards, two soldiers in a group of three Germans, two cooks of three Frenchmen, and two whoremongers among three Englishmen."

"I can agree with that."

"Doesn't it seem to you we could go on forever?"

"Absolutely. There have never been so many sharp words uttered about any other nation."

"Because no other people occupied half the planet for so long."

"Which means it's time we praise and congratulate each other."

"As Englishmen?"

"What else?"

"Permit me a small question."

"Go ahead."

"How do you know things different peoples have said about the English so well? That's not your business as a doctor."

"As a professor of diction at the Royal Academy of Dramatic Art, that's probably not your business either, at least professionally. So I redirect the question."

"Has the time come when it makes sense to lay our cards on the table?"

"I think it has."

"Well, begin."

"Why don't you begin?"

"Do you have a coin in your pocket?"

"We're not going to do a toss. You begin. In exchange, I'll tell you something you don't know when we're done."

"I know that I know nothing. You'll probably tell me everything that Socrates himself didn't know."

"Something concrete."

"Alright. I'm on my way to Brisbane, where I plan to take part in the world championship of quotation aficionados, and win."

"And thereby entice back your wife, who's now happy with her black Jesus on the west coast of Ireland?"

"I doubt that will entice her."

"But those things are temporary. Women realize much sooner than men that they have made a mistake."

"I won't take her back."

"Think it over."

"And you? How do you know all those sayings about the English?"

"I'm also on my way to Brisbane. Not to compete, but to assist my son, who's sitting four rows ahead nursing the hope of winning after the long training we've done."

"Your son is my competitor?"

"He's far from being the only one. 420 participants from all over the world have registered."

"It will begin with preliminary competitions, and only ten finalists will fight for the prize."

"It will be stressful. But the very fact that the University of Brisbane announced such a competition is something worthy of praise, don't you think?"

"Why?"

"Because mankind has reached the point where everything is just a quotation. All the books that come out in a miniscule number or millions of copies are only deftly concealed quotations of literary works that have appeared in the last three thousand years. Technology is probably indeed developing, but spiritually—with some variations, of course—we've been repeating ourselves for two thousand years."

"Everything in the world is just quotation?"

"Show me something totally original."

"Leaving aside technology?"

"Let's say."

"This game of ours."

"You don't mean to say that we're sitting next to each other by pure coincidence?"

"I don't know. Besides matter, coincidence is the most widespread and unavoidable thing in the universe. On the level of quantum mechanics, the universe is continually renewing and maintaining itself only by repeating random collisions of certain particles. The two of us coincidentally finding ourselves seated together on a flight to Sydney is a trifle compared to the existence of the universe."

"I would use simpler words."

"For example."

"You're a doctor employed by the Charing Cross Hospital in London. My wife worked there as a nurse until recently."

"The one who left you for the black Jesus?"

"No, I invented that just now. Don't forget that I work with actors at the Royal Academy."

"And?"

"Actors play. Roles. I learned from them that it's sometimes good to pretend."

"And tell a lie."

"Not necessarily a lie, but an approximate truth."

"To convince people that what you're acting is not a play but something that is really taking place."

"Well, I would formulate it differently, but yes, something like that."

"And?"

"Why don't you admit that you, too, are acting?"

"Doesn't half the world do that?"

"That has nothing to do with us and the fact that we're sitting next to each other by coincidence."

"And you think that I'm responsible for that coincidence?"

"No, I'm responsible. After twenty slaps that brought blood from her nose, my spouse, your lover, furnished me information about the day you were planning to fly to Australia, along with the flight and seat number."

"Are you joking?"

"As you know, she wanted to go with you. You actually reserved the flight and seats."

"After all I've heard, I can't deny it."

"Well, she gave me the information, and for a large surcharge I changed the name on the ticket, and that's how I'm sitting next to you."

"Something like that is only possible in a spy novel."

"All the passengers on the plane are characters in novels, trite or complex, it doesn't matter at all, because of late there's no noticeable difference between them."

"But you said you're going to the world championship of quotation aficionados, like my son."

"I made that up. I knew what your intention was in going to Australia, and I opened a few books and memorized a thing or two."

"But that's a devilish plan."

"Didn't I tell you I wanted vengeance?"

"On me or the world?"

"The world is the same as you. Lying, cheating, and hostile to me. By taking vengeance on you, I take vengeance on the world."

"And how do you intend to take vengeance on me?"

"I told you."

"You brought a bomb on the plane?"

"Don't dare laugh at idiots. You always have to take them seriously."

"That sounds like a quotation. Who said it?"

"I did."

"I still suspect that you're joking."

"You took advantage of my wife's trust. You used your position as head of the department to pressure her with veiled threats until she relented. A true Englishman. And the story about Jewish ancestors from Ukraine was a lie."

"That was part of the game we were playing. You fed me a few lies yourself."

"Only as part of my vengeance."

"I beg you. We're living in the twenty-first century."

"Exactly. In the century when innocent people are beheaded in Syria and Iraq, while real criminals, like the CEOs of international corporations, swagger around in freedom."

"And I'm guilty of all of that."

"You caused my wife, all I had in the world, to be estranged from me. I decided that the world is sick. That I'm the world. That I'm sick."

"Where did you get the idea vengeance will cure you?"

"I personally may be curable, but now that I've become the world, there's no help for me."

"And when will the bomb explode and kill 500 innocent people?"

"The bomb won't destroy the plane. What do you take me for? Another proof of contempt you feel for your lover's husband. For a loving man like me to be a mass murderer? I fastened the bomb, the little bomb, the bomblette, or call it an explosive device, to the bottom of your son's seat. I can detonate it by pressing a certain number on the cell phone in my right pocket. It won't kill him. But he'll certainly end up in a wheelchair."

"What did my son do to you?"

"Nothing. But isn't that the most pleasurable part of vengeance? That the victim is innocent?"

"No offence, but you're mentally ill. I have friends, experts who can help you."

"But no one can help your son."

"Steward!"

The head steward is nearby and quickly responds.

"Sir?" he discretely leans over to the doctor.

"My neighbor claims that he put a small bomb under my son's seat, and when it detonates, he will be an invalid."

The head steward remains unfazed. He calmly turns to the jilted husband. "Is that true, sir?"

"I didn't say anything of the kind. The gentleman just invented it, because we disagreed about something."

"All the same we must check it out."

"I'm surprised you haven't sounded an alarm."

"Where is your son sitting?" the head steward looks at the doctor.

"There, by the window, the red-haired one in glasses."

The head steward goes aft, disappears behind a

curtain, and after a while returns along the aisle on the other side with a corpulent white man who can't hide the suppressed worry on his boxer's face. They stop next to an elegant lady and two young men sitting in the same row, with the red-haired one in glasses by the window.

The head steward asks—more like orders—the three to leave their seats. All three comply without a word. The corpulent guy with a boxer's face, the only white man in the crew, opens a lighter, gets on his knees, with difficulty forces his way between the two rows, and carefully examines the bottom of the window seat. He removes the life belt and once more carefully feels and examines it. Then he replaces the life belt and crawls on his knees back to the aisle. He gets to his feet, looks at the head steward, and shakes his head. The head steward apologizes to the three passengers and invites them to retake their seats. He and the boxer head aft. After some time the head steward returns to the doctor and jilted husband by the right aisle.

"Gentlemen, jokes like may have been allowed on planes thirty years ago. Not any more. I request that you hand me your passports. Upon arrival you'll be interviewed by the police."

"Pleasant feeling?" the jilted husband turns to the doctor with a malicious smile.

"You'll be punished, not me." the doctor responds calmly.

"You already have been," says the man who can't bear Englishmen. "You've burdened yourself with my wife. Can't tell you how glad I am about all that awaits you."

15.

Side Effects

"Grandma, what's wrong? You're all pale."

"Aren't I always?"

"But not like that! Are you afraid of flying?"

"Not at all. For a woman my age, it's all the same—in the air, on the ground, or on the bottom of the sea."

"Grandma, you're still young."

"At ninety? Maybe something's wrong with you?"

"A lot is wrong with me, granny, even though I'm three times younger than you."

"I'm confused. Time… is not on my side."

"Did it pass too quickly?"

"No, lately it's dragging, but…"

"What?"

"If the time changes from hour to hour, as you said…"

"Yes, because we're flying east. It would also be changing if we were flying west."

"Why does it change?"

"I think it would be too hard to explain that, grandma."

"I don't know how to schedule my pills. Because I have to take each one at a certain hour."

"You take pills?"

"Do you know any ninety-year old women who don't take pills?"

"Why, for what?"

"Ask the doctor who prescribed them. And she drove

home that I have to take each one precisely at the same hour."

"You mean you take different ones? At different hours?"

"Eight different ones. Some together, some four hours apart, and some ten hours apart."

"Grandma, the doctor is going to kill you."

"Be a good girl and don't say foolish things. You're the only one on this plane I can depend on."

"But, grandma, eight different pills a day--why, for what?"

"I don't recall any longer. I only know which one I have to take at what hour. Now I don't even know that."

"I'll count for you."

"How will you do that?"

"Look, every so often there's information on the screen in front of you about what time it is there, where we departed from. That's our time. And what time it is at our present location, and there, where we're headed.

"I don't see anything."

"I'll let you know. What time do you have to take the first pills?"

"At seven in the morning."

"Our time?"

"Who else's?"

"But grandma, our seven o'clock is long passed. It's now nine-thirty."

"What does that mean? That I missed it, or it's too soon?"

"Grandma, you missed it. You probably took them just before we took off but don't remember."

"I packed them all up last night and put them in the luggage."

"In the luggage? The luggage is in the belly of the plane, and you won't see it until we arrive in Sydney!"

"No, in this one. In my bag, the one up above."

"Shall I give it to you?"

"That would be good of you."

The granddaughter opens the compartment above the seats, pulls out a black bag, and opens it."

"Jesus, grandma, you're transporting an entire drugstore!"

"I have only pills, my passport, medical insurance, and the address of a person to be informed in the event of my death."

"Oh, grandma…"

"That person is you."

"Not the aunt in Sydney we're going to visit?"

"Hah!"

"Which are the ones you forgot to take at seven?"

"These. What are they called. I can't see without my glasses."

"Crestor. Why are you taking them?"

"To lower my cholesterol."

"Cholesterol! Grandma, *everyone* your age has high cholesterol, but no one dies from it!"

"Thousands of people my age die all over the world every day."

"But not from cholesterol, grandma, but because they reached the age when people die. Most people die even earlier."

"My doctor says I have to take them, so I take them. Give me one, with a little water."

"I pressed the button, the light went on, and the stewardess will come with water."

"I don't understand at all. Give me the pill."

"Grandma, we have to wait for the water."

"It will be too late."

"A couple hours difference means nothing with most pills."

"My doctor said…"

"Grandma, did the doctor warn you about the pills'

possible side effects?"

"No, she said they're fine, only I have to take them."

"Do you have headaches, stomach pains, constipation, a feeling of fatigue, muscle pain, or dizziness?"

"For twenty years."

"On account of these pills?"

"I've been taking the pills for five years."

"Do you know they can cause diabetes?"

"I have that. I take pills for it, too. Every day at eleven. What time is it?"

"Grandma, this is terrible. How many different things do you take pills for?"

"Ten. Eleven. Maybe twelve."

"I can't believe…"

"I have a list of when I have to take which one, but I left it at home on the table."

"Grandma, listen. Pills aren't only medicine. They're also poison. Did one doctor prescribe all of them?"

"She's exceptionally pleasant. Whenever I say that I have a pain somewhere, she immediately writes a prescription."

"Oh, grandma… your doctor is putting you in mortal danger."

"Who's not in mortal danger at ninety?"

"That's another thing. You can't just take these pills."

"But that's the way it always was—I just took them. With a glass of water at such and such an hour."

"That's the problem. Behind the medicine your rightly trust is a greedy pharmacological industry. Look, grandma, there's no sense in explaining this to you. You wouldn't understand anything I'd say."

"You don't trust doctors. I don't either."

"And all the same you take all those pills."

"I know they won't help me. But they can't hurt me either. Except when I get diarrhea now and again. And you can imagine how quickly I can get to the bathroom at my age."

"Do you ever have a swollen face? Lips? Tongue? Throat?"

"Not that I've noticed."

"Do you have trouble swallowing or breathing?"

"It's hard to swallow and harder to breathe. But that's been for a while."

"What about coughing? Fever?"

"Once a year, when I get a cold."

"Grandma, what about goose bumps, hand and foot pain, depression, trouble sleeping, constant muscle weakness, memory loss, or jaundice?"

"You mean I have to take pills for all that?"

"No, grandma, those are all possible side effects of the pills you take to lower your cholesterol! How high is your cholesterol?"

"I never forget that. I try to but I can't. My cholesterol is 5.6 of something called mmm. I have no idea what that means."

"Are you joking? Then why is the doctor prescribing you pills?"

"She says that science is progressing and the latest is that I should have 5.0. So, she says, I'd better take the pills."

"Show me what else you take. Show them to me."

"They're all in that plastic bag."

"Metformin, repaglinide, and akarboza. These are for diabetes, these you have to take. But diabetes was caused, grandma, by taking pills to lower your cholesterol."

"Why are you yelling at me?"

"Sorry. All this makes me mad. Why are you taking omeprazole?"

"My doctor said it's for acid. The other pills give me stomach acid, and the heartburn kills me."

"You take some pills only because you take others?"

"I'm not a doctor. I was a housewife all my life."

"Do you have any idea about omeprazole's side effects? Overall poor feeling and lack of energy, hives, itchiness. Agitation, confusion, or malaise. Fractures of the hip, wrist, or backbone. Serious kidney problems, kidney failure, and brain fever. Hallucinations."

"But the acid is very bad, it comes up my esophagus, into my throat, and even my mouth."

"What else do we have here? Indapamide. For reducing blood pressure. When is the last time they checked it? What was it?"

"A month ago. I think it was 139 over 85."

"That's normal for your age!"

"Of course, I take pills."

"What was it before you started taking them?"

"How would I know? I've been taking the pills for ten years. Some for twenty."

"Excuse me, grandma, but I'm surprised you're still alive. And what's this? Lexaurin. Bromazepam. That's a sedative, grandma!"

"I can't sleep without it."

"Oh, grandma…"

"What is it, my dear?"

"You know what we're going to do? We're going to put all these pills back in the bag, the we'll put the bag back in the overhead compartment, and you won't take any more pills."

"Then I'll die."

"Except the ones for diabetes. You have to take those."

"At what time?"

"We'll check. The others you won't touch any more. In Sydney I'll take you for all kinds of examinations, and ethical doctors will tell you that you don't need most of these pills, if any of them."

"Who will pay for the examinations?"

"My aunt."

"Well, I've got to see that. Have you ever in your life met her?"

"No."

"I have to warn you that she's not like your mom."

"I like *you* most of all. That's why I want you to live another twenty years."

"If you really liked me, you wouldn't want that."

***

"Grandma, how do you feel?"

"What? Sorry, I fell asleep."

"Are you alright?"

"Insofar as that's possible at my age."

"I mean since you didn't take the pills that you were supposed to."

"I didn't?"

"No, we agreed that you wouldn't, because you don't need them. Are you alright? Do you feel normal?"

"I don't know anymore what's normal."

"Does anything hurt? Do you feel sick? Are you dizzy?"

"Everything hurts, I feel as sick as if I'd eaten an uncooked mouse, and I'm as dizzy as if I were in a plane above the clouds."

"You *are* above the clouds, grandma. We're rocking a little. We ran into mild turbulence, but at least it won't last long."

"I know. A few more months, maybe a year, and I'll be gone."

"Grandma, you really worry me. Do you feel well?"

"Why?"

"Because I didn't give you a whole slew of pills that the doctor says you have to take regularly."

"I feel like usual."

"No worse?"

"I don't know. Maybe I feel so poorly that I can no longer tell whether I feel worse."

"Grandma, you're not going to take those pills anymore."

"My doctor will be very angry."

"Tell her you're taking them. Let her prescribe them. But you just throw them in the toilet."

"That's not honest. I'd rather tell her I won't take them anymore."

"That's fine, too. But I'm afraid she'll force you."

"The only way someone can force a person my age to do something is by hitting her on the head with a hammer."

"Bravo, grandma."

"Are you still in school? I know you told me, but you understand… at my age…"

"I studied pharmaceutical medicine. I quit in the second year."

"Why?"

"I saw that pharmaceuticals are a conspiracy against human well being."

"I'm sorry… I can't take things in anymore… what does that mean?"

"The means that the pharmaceutical industry wants to generate more profit. So they produce more and more pills for ever more illnesses that doctors think up."

"Aren't doctors the only people in the world you can trust?"

"No, grandma, doctors are no different from most people."

"But my…"

"The best are the ones who devote the most time to you and prescribe the least number of pills."

"Will something happen to me? Something bad?"

"Why?"

"Because I'm no longer taking pills that I should."

"Grandma, only one thing can happen. You'll feel better."

"I haven't noticed so far."

"You soon will."

"Now I really don't know anymore who to trust. My doctor or my niece, who didn't finish pharmaceutical school."

"I'm not your niece, grandma, I'm your granddaughter."

"Of course. It's hard to know at my age, when your relatives multiply, who's who. You're my granddaughter. Of course. And Mary in Australia we're going to visit is what? Your mom?"

"My aunt, grandma."

"Since strangers keep coming through the walls into my living room, I don't know anymore who is who."

"Strangers are coming through the walls?"

"They're very nice. All gentlemen. They come, sit on the couch, and look at me. Then they get up and leave without a word."

"When did they start appearing?"

"Here, on the plane, it seems to me."

"But there's no living room here, grandma."

"Sure there is. I take my living room with me wherever I go. And my sofa. I couldn't sit anywhere else."

"Grandma, did this start when you were supposed to take one of the pills from your bag or before?"

"I don't know. It just started."

"You know what, grandma, those are the side effects of withdrawal. They appear when you stop taking pills your body has grown used to. It will pass. And then you'll feel as good as ever before."

"That's how I'll feel when I die. Maybe right here on the plane."

"Grandma, don't be silly."

"No, I really want to. I'm closer to God here. I'm

only a few steps away from Him."

"Grandma, please."

"Where did you say we're flying? To your aunt's?"

"To you youngest daughter's, grandma. To my dead mom's sister. Your youngest daughter is getting married. At the age of fifty."

"She's already been married, twice!'

"This will be the third time, grandma."

"I was married only once, and that was more than enough."

"I'm not going to marry at all."

"Smart. A husband always wants to be smarter than you."

"Maybe I'll marry a woman, grandma."

"That's impossible."

"Nowadays it is."

"For heaven's sake, which of you will have a child?"

"That's the easiest thing. You go to a singles' bar one night, and you have a child. It could be that we'll each have one."

"Might I take one of the pills you said I shouldn't and didn't give me?"'

"Which one, grandma? Omeprazole? Bromazepam?"

"I don't know. Something to clear my head. The world seems more and more strange."

"How long have you been taking bromazepam?"

"I have no idea. A long time. Maybe my whole life."

"Three months are enough to see negative effects."

"It always calmed me down. And no one appeared in my living room through the wall."

"Grandma, I'm going to list for you the side effects of taking bromazepam."

"What are you talking about?"

"Fatigue, sleepiness, disorientation, dizziness."

"I'm ninety years old, my dear. How old are you? Twenty-five?"

"Twenty-three, grandma."

"If you had everything you listed, you should be worried. It's normal for me."

"Headaches, difficulty concentrating, forgetfulness?"

"All of that. For twenty years already."

"Lax muscles, low blood pressure, confusion, erratic behavior, jumbled speech, blurred vision, constipation, jaundice, skin blemishes."

"All of that, as I recall."

"You're not jaundiced, grandma, because your eyes aren't yellow. But you have all the rest. And all of it is from taking bromazepam long-term. You wouldn't need it if you weren't taking all the other pills."

"I'm so glad to having my personal doctor traveling with me."

"What else do you have? Nitroglycerin. Do you have angina? Do you have heart pain?"

"Of course. Severe."

"Every day?"

"No. Only when I recall what I missed in life."

"Then why did you doctor prescribe this dangerous drug? From now on, you won't take it."

"Right, but how will I feel without it?"

"Do you want me to read the side effects?"

"I'd rather you didn't. As it is I'm getting the sense that my entire life has been one big side effect. But I don't know from what."

"Grandma, if no one else will, I'll defend you against the effects of the poisons that avaricious pharmacologists call medicine. I hope you understand me."

"But right now I'm very tired and would like to sleep."

She makes herself comfortable in her seat and closes her eyes.

"Grandma?"

Grandma doesn't reply.

***

"Grandma, how are you?"

The old woman doesn't respond. Her granddaughter shakes her.

"Grandma, are you alright?"

"Grrr... Hmmm..."

"How do you feel?"

"What?"

"Do you feel alright?"

"I don't know."

"Do you feel better than usual?"

"Possibly."

"You see, that's because you're not taking harmful pills."

"What?"

"Everything's alright, grandma. You'll be well before long."

"I'm sleepy."

"Just close your eyes. Take a rest."

"'Hmmm..."

"It won't bother you if I keep talking?"

"No..."

"You don't have to answer. Just listen."

"Brrrr..."

"I have to tell you a few things."

"Yes..."

"I have quite a few problems. And you're the only one I trust."

"Hmmm..."

"I didn't finish my pharmacology program. I quit my studies, because I didn't want to take part in poisoning people with artificial substances in the name of profit."

"Rrrr..."

"It's a matter of principle, grandma."

"Hmmm…"

"*No* is always an easier answer than *yes*, isn't it, grandma? Because *yes* binds and sets conditions that demand a reason and intention. *No* is simply *no*: blow it out your ass, get lost, I can't stand you, I'm too good for you, I'm not interested in you, I don't have time, leave me alone."

"Gggg…?"

"But tell me, grandma, is *no* always bad? Is it necessary to say *yes* sometimes?" Doesn't that mean that I relinquish the right to judge and choose?"

"Eeeggghhh…"

"I knew you'd understand me."

"Oooohhrrr…"

"You probably guessed that I'm talking about boys who court me. Not to marry me, but for something else. You probably know what I mean."

"Nnnnn…"

"So far I haven't said yes. Not once. And you know why? Because I can't say there's a boy in the whole wide world who I could say I like. And there never will be. I value myself too highly. No boy should ever imagine he can win me as a prize for some cheap words."

"Rrrr…"

"I knew you'd agree with me. But if you'd like to sleep, go ahead. You don't have to listen."

"Dddd-nn-mmmm…"

"I'll confess something else. I didn't quit my studies. They expelled me, because I kept saying that all synthetic medicines are a part of a conspiracy on the part of world's real rulers to poison half the population. There're too many of us, grandma. There's not enough food or water, and more than half of us have to be killed. They showed me the door just because I doggedly insisted that we have to return to natural medicines. And I even offered to open and head a special department for very modest pay. Grandma?"

Grandma doesn't reply.

"You're obviously asleep. That's good, because you won't hear what I'm going to tell you now. Wouldn't you rather hear?"

Grandma doesn't answer.

"That's right, I won't wake you up. I suffered a terrible injustice, grandma. More terrible than anything that's ever happened to anyone in the world."

"Aaaagggghhhhhrrrr"

"When I put up a tent in front of the school, thinking to organize an educational workshop I called 'Back to Natural Medicine,' they forcibly removed me. You know where to? To the same institution my mom was at before she jumped from a sixth-floor balcony."

Grandma doesn't reply.

"They said I was sick. I secretly tossed all the medicine, as they call it there, into the toilet. And since I didn't swallow one pill, after a while they told me I was fine and let me go."

Grandma doesn't reply.

"It was only two months ago I could breathe easy again. Otherwise I couldn't have gone with you on this trip. I know how much you want to see your youngest daughter one more time before you die. Even though, as you said, you can't stand her."

Grandma doesn't reply.

"Grandma, are you alright?" She shakes her. "Grandma, wake up. You're all pale. Why are you eyes open so wide?" She gives her another, stronger shake.

Grandma wavers and slumps over, motionless, her head against the window.

"Stewardess, my grandma won't wake up! Can you help me?" She turns back to her grandma and starts pounding her with her fists. "Grandma! Wake up! Don't do this to me!"

The stewardess hurries over. "What's wrong?"

"My grandma won't wake up."

"Oh my God!"

The stewardess rushes down the aisle and returns with the head steward. He leans across the young lady towards the grandmother and looks at her closely.

He turns around and loudly yells, "Doctor, sir! I apologize for taking your passport. We have a problem here!"

The doctor on the other side of the plane gets up and approaches via the aisle around the restrooms to where the incident is taking place. As soon as he sees the old lady's unusual appearance, he leans towards her past the young woman and puts a finger on the artery in her neck. This goes on for a while. Then he checks the pulse on her wrist. Then he uses both hands to close her mouth, which had remained open.

"The lady is dead," he says.

"Now this," the head steward shakes his head. Then he glances sharply at the young woman.

"That's my grandma!" she shouts.

"You're traveling together?" asks the doctor.

"The pills killed her! You doctors killed her! Every last one of you will go to jail!"

"Was the lady taking pills?"

"Tons of pills! Thanks to the conspiracy you're part of. But I wouldn't give her any. Not one. They should have given her only natural medicine."

"What was the last pill she should have taken?"

"Nitroglycerin."

"Did the lady have heart problems? Angina?"

"Do you have any idea what nitroglycerin is? An explosive! Should I give my grandmother something that men at war used to kill each other?"

"Just a minute. The lady was supposed to take nitroglycerin, and you didn't give it to her?"

"No, because it has too many side effects."

"Unfortunately I have to tell you that you killed your

grandmother."

"That's impossible! I'm a student of pharmacology."

The doctor turns to the head steward. "I can't do anything. From here on, things are in your hands."

"I'll inform the captain. Since we're approaching Singapore, he probably won't choose to make an emergency landing."

He hurries to the front of the plane.

"Can I return to my seat?"

"Of course. Thank you, doctor," says the stewardess.

Before leaving, the doctor turns once more to the old lady's granddaughter. "No offence, but you should be locked up."

"Not me, you!" screams the young woman so loudly that almost the whole plane hears her. "You, who are always lying that you're curing us, when in fact you're intentionally poisoning us!"

"Keep an eye on her," the doctor whispers to the stewardess.

16.

Pride Parade

"Can I read you something?"
"Right now, when I'm reading myself?"
"You're reading a newspaper; I'm reading a book."
"And?"
"You're reading news reports; I'm reading a story."
"So?"
"Stories are more interesting."
"Not all of them."
"You have to hear this. It's not long."
"Well, go ahead."
"Some Indian trains, especially long-distance expresses, have up to forty cars and besides countless pieces of luggage and their owners they also carry a multitude of stories and intrigues, personal traumas, tragedies, deception, dreams, and evil thoughts. If statistics are to be believed, on every train there's at least one serial killer, three robbers, ten thieves, five men traveling with women who aren't their wives, eight people who are mortally ill but don't know it, twenty girls who claim to be virgins but aren't, seven people who were robbed the day before, ten people who were wronged by the law, and so on and so forth... Isn't that interesting?"
"What are you reading?"
"A novel. *Now We Are Two*. Nice title, don't you think?"
"And why did you want to read me precisely that excerpt?"

"Don't you see?"
"What?"
"The parallel!"
"What parallel?"
"Doesn't the same thing go for this plane?"
"You mean there's a mass murderer among us?"
"Maybe even two."
"And five men traveling with women who aren't their wives?"
"You don't think it's possible?"
"Anything's possible. Maybe there're *three* murderers among us. And *twenty* robbers. And *thirty* mentally disturbed people. Maybe there's even a handful of normal, honest people on the plane. Even that's possible. And also most likely."
"Look at those three by the window on the other side. Two young guys and a girl in the middle."
"What's wrong with them?"
"I bet the girl is a whore, and one of the boys is her pimp."
"Which one?"
"The bigger one. The messy, long-haired one."
"What about the other?"
The one with the shaved head? Maybe his brother. But he's a good kind, less evil than the pimp, who is constantly shuffling his feet and waiving his arms."
"How do you know he's a good kind?"
"He's calm. Introspective. You can tell by his face that he's not violent."
"What if he's the murderer?"
"That's not possible. You can tell a murderer by his features."
"How many murderers have you known?"
"I'm talking in general…"
"If that were really true, the police would arrest all the murderers before they killed anyone. And then there

wouldn't be any murders."

"But the girl is for sure a whore."

"Why?"

"Look at her eyes. The rings. The jaded look. Fear. All spent whores, even the young ones, have a special expression of exhaustion on their faces."

"I'd call it sleep deprivation."

"Of course. Night work."

"What about the murderer? See him anywhere?"

"Not in the immediate vicinity. I should take a walk down the aisle, from the nose of the plane to the tail."

"Go on."

"I will. As soon as the flight attendant moves the cart."

"You can read your book until then. And I'll read my paper." He again unfolds it.

"I'm fascinated by how many different people can come together in the same place by pure chance. And each one is hiding something. Or is silent. Or pretends to be sleeping. Or is arguing with a neighbor. Or is pressing against him. Or is staring at the screen in front of him. That's the majority."

"People are bored. They're watching movies."

"Look at that one, two rows up on the right. He's been staring at the flight map for several hours already. I'd understand if the plane icon were moving, but it's not. It's in the same place the whole time."

"So we're not flying? We've stopped in midair?"

"It's moving, but not so he can see it. Of course you see it, but only after an hour or so do you notice a centimeter of progress. And he's been staring at the screen as if bewitched. As if he believes he can move the icon ahead by force of will and thus the plane."

"Why don't you let people entertain themselves however they like?"

"That's not entertainment; it's a sickness."

"What's it called?"

"I remember doing that myself a while ago. I was flying from London to Chicago, staring at the screen the whole time. And when we were flying over the lower part of Greenland, it seemed to me we hung in the same place for four hours. I'm not joking. We hung in the same place for four hours. And the same thing when we were flying over the Great Lakes towards Chicago. It seemed we weren't moving at all."

"And why were you flying to Chicago?"

"Why do you care?"

"Just because."

"Look…"

"And now all of a sudden we have secrets?"

"No. I was going to a gay parade."

"Without me."

"John, that was before we met!"

"Are you sure?"

"Don't tell me you're suddenly jealous of things I did before we met? Because then I have the same right."

"I was just curious."

"I feel like you're interrogating me."

"Forget it. I didn't say anything. After all, we're going to a gay parade in Sydney. This time together. I'd say it's cause to be happy."

"Absolutely. But stop digging into my past, alright? Have I ever asked you how many blow jobs you gave before we met?"

"Good thing you didn't."

"Why? Because the number would shock me?"

"Look, we said…"

"Right. We don't have pasts. alright? We were innocent when we met. The question is whether we stay that way."

"I have good intentions."

"I do, too."

"Can I read my paper now?"

"No, because we haven't finished with the things we were talking about."

"Which ones?"

"How that idiot over there has been fixated on the plane icon since we took off."

"You said you did the same thing."

"But I stopped. It lasted a long time, but in the end I realized it was a technical mistake. The icon simply jumps ahead every so often; it doesn't follow the plane's actual flight."

"And that cured it?"

"Forever."

"And now you no longer follow the flight on the screen?"

"I only check it. Every so often. To see where we're at. Want me to check?"

"No."

"I can see it from here on that poor idiot's screen. Know where we're at? Somewhere over eastern Iran."

"I hope they are not testing ground to air missiles."

"The one behind us, haven't you heard him? Not directly behind us, these two ladies are Finnish, but the one behind them. The one with glasses."

"What about him?"

"The lady who was sitting next to him is terrified of flying. And he was describing to her in great detail all the plane crashes that have happened so far."

"Sadist?"

"He claimed to be a therapist, curing people of phobias. Did you know that there are more than a hundred different phobias?"

"Maybe he is that statistical murderer from the average Indian train."

"Now you are making fun of me."

"Sorry."

"It's terrible to frighten someone who is afraid of flying with detailed descriptions of plane crashes and the numbers of victims. The lady demanded to be moved to another seat. And she was."

"Good."

"But now there is a really strange man sitting next to the therapist. Reminds me of an actor in a crime movie I saw not long ago."

"Sorry…what? I didn't hear that."

"Because you are completely confused by the falling shares on the stock market. How many have you got? Lost a lot of money?"

"I'll still be able to pay for our hotel. And for a few extras."

"I'm glad. But for once in your life agree with me. Scaring old ladies…"

"Yes, yes! You're eavesdropping! That's your problem. You eavesdrop and come to conclusions based on partial information. That's always been your problem."

"Thanks."

"Look… That's not what I meant. But there are a lot of conversations on such a long flight aboard such a large plane. Between acquaintances and strangers. Between friends and enemies."

"Actually not. Most people sleep, watch films, or sip wine. Only now and then do you hear words spoken. Isn't it normal to overhear them?"

"I don't hear anything."

"Because you don't listen. I do. I hope you won't forbid me to."

"Not at all. But at least you could consider the possibility that the two ladies behind us, who heaven knows why you took to be Finnish, might understand English.

"So?"

"I beg you! Can't you assume that in this case they've been listening to our conversation the whole time?

At least I'm quiet, while you've been almost yelling."

The younger one turns around to look between the seats. "Excuse me, ladies, do you understand English?"

"Nyet, nyet," says the older lady. "We from Ukraine, no speak English."

"Finnish, huh?" the older one turns to the younger.

"You can't expect me to know all languages."

The ladies behind them exchange glances and wink.

***

"You're not going to check where we are?"

"We're flying over India."

"How do you know?"

"I can see from the guy who's still staring at the screen. He must be really sick."

"Everyone on this plane is sick. Each in his own way."

"We are, too?"

"Since you're always buried in a book, you must have read *A Ship of Fools*."

"No."

"Someone could write a novel called *A Plane of Fools*."

"Aren't you exaggerating a little?"

"You think most people on this plane are mentally fit?"

"To some extent."

"Are you sure there's such a thing as mental health?"

"By the logic of things, those who treat the mentally ill must be healthy."

"Some would say it's the abnormal treating the abnormal."

"Where did you read that? In the *Financial Times*?"

"Are we healthy?"

"Mentally at least."

"In seventy-two countries, we would get the death penalty, a public flogging, or a long jail term for doing what we do."

"That means that mentally ill people are in charge of seventy-two countries."

"Most heterosexuals think that we gays are sick. Of course, they won't admit that publicly."

"That means that the majority of heterosexuals are sick."

"What about the countries which allow same-sex marriage and even adoption?"

"Some would say that mentally ill people are in charge of those countries, too."

"Do you still think that gays are something special?"

"I'm not saying that, but we have to fight for our rights."

"Against whom?"

"Against everyone who denies us our rights."

"How about people who deny rights to women, the handicapped, blind, unemployed, children and members of other tribes or parties?"

"They have to fight for their rights. And I support them if they do."

"In your thoughts?"

"Morally. That's the only way I can."

"Why? They should fight for everyone's rights. You've simplistically divided the world into two halves—gays and heterosexuals. As if that were the world's biggest problem."

"Excuse me, but… what are you trying to say?"

"That the world is much more complex than you imagine."

"As I imagine?"

"Yes, you."

"It seems to me that you're trying to say something else."

"That is."

"That I'm mentally inferior and therefore not the best partner for you."

"I realized that a long time ago, but that doesn't mean you're not a good partner for me."

"Why not?"

"You're good looking. You take care of your body. You're great at sex. You're super as far as those things are concerned. And most of all you're young."

"In short, I'm just your sex toy."

"That's how most relationships are, including between heterosexuals."

"Since you're a wealthy stockbroker, and I'm a poor student, you're convinced that you're buying me. That I'm your whore."

"Please."

"But that's the way it is, no?"

"Even if it is, what's so bad? The main thing is we have good—even excellent—time in bed."

"Never before have you humiliated me. Now, high above the clouds, you suddenly have the courage. I didn't know you're a sadist."

"Far from it, but facts are facts."

"I could tell you quite a few things about you that bother me."

"Be my guest."

"I'd rather not. We're sitting together another twelve hours. And what will happen in Sydney? We have a room reserved in the same hotel. One room."

"Those are the facts. But they're unconnected to the things about me that bother you. Which ones? You think it's honest not to tell me?"

"I'd rather not be left without a roof over my head in Sydney."

"And money."

"I knew you'd say that."

"You're accusing me in advance of behavior that I'm incapable of. I'm sorry you're doing this, but it's a habit of yours and one of the things that bothers me about you."

"One of the things?"

"You promised to tell me what bothers you about me."

"You're conceited."

"Really? I see myself as one of the most modest people in the world."

"That's characteristic of narcissists."

"I'm that, too? Anything else?"

"You don't value me. You're convinced that you're so educated, but in fact you've read ten times fewer books than I have, even though you're twice as old."

"How do you know?"

"Ever since we met, you read only the *Financial Times*. As if it were the Bible. You read some articles three times. Instead of picking up some book."

"What if I read most of the books—even more than you—by the time I was your age?"

"I doubt it. And if you did, they were books about finance, economics, and things like that."

"Well I didn't study psychology."

"It shows."

"And who's conceited now?"

"Sorry."

"What else about me bothers you?"

"You're too proud of your money."

"Anything else?"

"The way you introduce me to friends, acquaintances, and former lovers."

"Always politely and praising you."

"Exactly, like a trophy."

"I'm sorry you take my desire to present you in the best light so wrongly."

"And then people say, 'Oh, look at him, he orders up

a new one every month, he has a lot of money, no surprise, he works in the stock exchange.'"

"Jealousy will always find its way into words."

"How does he get rid of them, some of them ask themselves."

"Did I ever indicate I want to get rid of you?"

"You know what else bothers me about you?"

"Be merciless."

"That you're bald."

"Really? The most attractive men in the world were bald. Yul Brynner. Bruce Willis. Do you have any idea how many handsome fellows there are who shave their heads?"

"You're not going to claim you're handsome?"

"I know I'm an average looking man with an occupation many envy. I know you're much more handsome than I, but besides having finished three years of college, you haven't done bugger all in life. And if you think I don't deserve you just on account of your looks, consider the fact that most people are attracted by something else entirely in a partner."

"For example?"

"Character. Depth of soul. Enthusiasm. Openness. Success."

"And you have all that."

"It was clearly only my money that attracted you."

"I don't know any more what drew me to you in the beginning, but we're now talking about what I don't like in you."

"Go on."

"From the very start I didn't like your body odor. Even when you get out of the shower, you smell somehow sour, moldy."

"But that hasn't bothered you the past three months."

"It did. I didn't dare tell you."

"You were afraid I'd stop paying the rent for your studio and taking you with me on trips around the world."

"Possibly."

"Then you really are a whore who sells himself for material gain."

"What do you want? For me to confess eternal love here above the clouds?"

"I've known for a long time that you suck my bank account much more intensively than my dick. But that didn't bother me as long as you at least pretended to like me."

"I pretended?"

"Don't think for a minute I didn't know that from the start."

"But still…"

"Yes, I still got involved with you, because I simply liked you. I also knew that you didn't really like me, and the time would come when we would face up to that. But I didn't know it would happen right here, on a flight to Australia, out of the blue."

"I have no idea how we arrived at this."

"Nor do I. But clearly the subconscious is at work."

"Actually, most of what I told you isn't at all true."

"Will you now try to convince me that it was revenge for the offence to your dignity, which unfortunately I can't recall."

"You're always treating me like I'm beneath you."

"I hadn't noticed."

"As if *Ana Karenina* were beneath the *Financial Times*."

"In fact it is, but that's not my fault."

"The superior can never be beneath the inferior."

"Except when it's necessary to pay for expensive hotel rooms and buy plane tickets from London to Australia."

"In that case as well, the inferior is beneath the superior. I admit I don't deserve you. I don't know why I was so awful to you. Will you forgive me?"

A short silence.

"We'll have to talk about another such thing or two."

"Let's."

"Not now. Later. When we've carefully considered our relationship."

"You're not going to leave me in the lurch when we get to Sydney?"

"Are you afraid?"

"A little for sure."

"Now I do see that I've chosen the wrong partner."

"I have certain mental problems I didn't dare tell you about. But now I will."

"I know you have problems. You're a fag."

"Excuse me, but…"

"Your problem is that you're ashamed of it. And that's your only problem."

17.

Turbulence

"What are you thinking about?"
"What do you think?"
"About what's soon going to happen?"
"You got it."
"I hope you won't disappoint me."
"You know very well where we come from and what we are."
"In our tribe, a brother has never disappointed a brother."
"Or a son his father and mother."
"Or a group member other group members."
"Especially not a group like we started and belong to heart and soul."
"Even though many people will condemn our act."
"Because they are blind and think only of themselves. We have to force them to open their eyes."
"In any case, there's no future for us in this world."
"I think the head steward suspects us."
"Why?"
"He was talking with that white man before, who is obviously Security, and they were cautiously looking our way."
"Maybe because I tried going up the stairs to first class."
"When?"
"A little while ago, when I was going to the restroom."

"Extremely stupid. Why did you do that?"

"I wanted to see that monster. That criminal who has all the laws on his side. That destroyer of the planet. That... I don't have words for him."

"But you saw him. We were going to kill him back in London."

"He slipped away. He was surrounded by bodyguards."

"Another reason not to go look at him in first class."

"I wanted to see his face up close."

"Why?"

"To see if there's anything human in it. Even a trace."

"Listen, brother. Sometimes you do things I wouldn't expect. And worse. Often you even think on your own."

"I'm struggling with that. In general, successfully, but not all the time."

"Since we're a group, bound to a sacred purpose, we can only think as a group."

"It's hard, because we can't see into each other's heads, much less hearts."

"What are you saying?"

"I want to be honest. Brother to brother. No matter what we've decided on."

"The group decided. We just offered to do the deed."

"You offered first. Then you convinced me."

"You're telling me that now you have second thoughts?"

"No, I don't. Only now and then I get an uneasy feeling about soon being dead, along with all the rest."

"Fear of death?"

"A little."

"More than of life on Earth, where the robbers of the world trample you as if you were less than a worm?"

"I'm afraid as a person, not as a member of a group that has decided the world needs a radical warning of what a handful of people can do to it."

"The world has to get that message in the name of all people."

"Even of those who will die with us?"

"That will make the message stronger."

"Even though more than half of the people on this plane have never heard of the forests on Sumatra?"

"We will remind the world that the primeval forests produce the oxygen people need to survive. If we destroy the forests, we will suffocate."

"I read a prediction. In the coming fifteen years, the worst deforestation will be on the Amazon, the Atlantic primeval forest, Borneo, Cerrado, Choco-Darien, the valleys in the Congo, eastern Australia, the Mekong basin, New Guinea, and Sumatra."

"Our homeland. Doesn't that make our act all the more justified?"

"How?"

"Because then the whole world will hear about what some people are doing. And perhaps it will have an impact. Did you forget that the group has already prepared a message for the media?"

"I know, dear brother. I know it all."

"Then what's the problem?"

"The problem is I can't silence or totally kill the person in me. That's exactly why I wanted to see the face of our victim up close. To see if there's anything human in him. If there's anything good. If he's maybe just blinded. If it's still possible to change him. To convince him that what he's doing is wrong."

"I hope they didn't let you go up."

"No. They said that economy passengers are not allowed on the upper deck."

"That's right. Upstairs are those who are above us. Who don't want to meet us. Because we don't exist in their calculations. We're just a workforce for them. As much as they need us. The plane's pilot and co-pilot are in the cockpit, but upstairs, in first class, are the pilots of the world."

"You're right."

"Besides, you'll find something human in the faces of the worst criminals. Especially on the faces of those who are unaware of their crimes. And that's the greatest problem. That ones destroying the world aren't aware of what they're doing. As if they were drunk."

"And what we're preparing will sober them up?"

"Dear brother, you've started doubting. The time has come to pray."

"Which way do we have to face?"

"We're flying east. Mecca is behind us."

"But we can't pray here like we're supposed to."

"We'll turn around and kneel between the seats."

***

"Although…"

"What, dear brother? The prayers didn't help?"

"They did. I'm not worried about that. I'm thinking about something else."

"Go on."

"Our victim is not completely without good qualities."

"I believe that. Maybe he's nice to his wife and children. Maybe he spoils them with all the money he has at his disposal. Maybe he takes them on vacation twice a year to some expensive resort in the Caribbean. Maybe he even goes to Bali, where he makes some unfortunates happy with his dollars. Almost no one in the world is devoid of good qualities."

"What are ours?"

"Shall I list them."

"Please."

"We've been loyal to our father and mother's memory after they were burned alive in our house when the primeval forest caught fire just to profit three, maybe five people."

"Loyalty is a good quality."

"Even then, as children, we swore to avenge for that crime."

"And for the deaths of all the animals that perished in the fire."

"The thought of revenge accompanied us all the way to college in Jakarta and advanced studies in London."

"Is that a good quality?"

"It's called persistence. Faithfulness to ideas. And to God."

"I don't dare imagine that God thinks like we do, or that he should."

"What's going on with you?"

"I'm thinking."

"It's not good to think too much."

"I studied zoology and the richness of millions of different animals gives me millions of different thoughts. Don't demand of me to reduce them to a single one."

"There're millions of different people living in the world. So why are most people's thoughts reduced to one during wars?"

"That's something different."

"We're at war, dear brother. Have you forgotten?"

"No. But I think it's necessary to see a person even in an enemy. Since you studied forestry, you might be less aware of that than I am."

"As my younger brother, you have to obey me and allow me to lead you."

"I obey you, dear brother. But I have a right to my own thoughts. Have you forgotten that we're educated?"

"Loyalty to an older brother, and above all to the

group you belong to is the greatest good."

"The person sitting upstairs in first class tried to be good to us, at least in the context of his values."

"Are you joking? By means of bribes and agreements with the owners, he bought thousands of hectares of primeval forest along the Sungai Siak River, not far from where our parents died in an illegal burn. And the tiger our father loved to talk with died with them. Surely you're not now going to say you don't know what his plans are?"

"I know. First he'll cut the trees down and sell them all over the world as precious lumber. Then he'll plant palms for palm oil that he'll sell all over the world. And then he'll be so rich that he won't know how rich he is."

"So?"

"And then, in cahoots with domestic traitors, he'll probably privatize the water in all large Indonesian cities. That already happened in Jakarta."

"And the result?"

"The price of water increased tenfold, a poisonous rusty swill comes out of the pipes, while other pipes are dry."

"Great progress. That's what our victim is planning?"

"I don't know what he's planning, but he guaranteed you the position of director of deforestation and reforestation with palms, and he promised me support to open a zoo for housing endangered animals who will have lost their habitat."

"Why don't they destroy the cities and preserve some specimens of people in a people park?"

"Doesn't it seem to you there's a difference between people and animals?"

"Remember the tiger that used to come to our house on the edge of the primeval forest?"

"How couldn't I?"

"Mom was afraid of him, but dad brought him food."

"Isn't it beautiful that a person and a wild animal can become such good friends?"

"I watched them from a distance, and it often seemed to me that they were talking."

"I think they did."

"People and animals that have been living in the primeval forest for thousands of years sense who is a friend and who is an enemy."

"Mom didn't believe that."

"No. She often said to our father, 'don't be so trusting, the Sumatran tiger is a terrible beast. One of these times he'll attack you and devour you."

"Which didn't happen."

"No, something else happened."

"People attacked us and devoured us. And the animals and the primeval forest."

"Progressive people."

"They saw in us wild men, and they saw the animals as beasts."

"And the primeval forest and lumber and money."

"I didn't tell you this, but once I saw our father pat the tiger on the head. Then the tiger licked his face."

"That's exactly why I'd like to explain to you that the person who along with five hundred others is going to end up on the bottom of the ocean, still tried, within his limits, to be good to us."

"The French call that a *coup de grace*. If you're not completely dead, they shoot you in the back of the head."

"I'm sorry, brother, it seems to me you're no longer capable of judging for yourself because of blind loyalty to the group."

"And you say that as a younger brother to his elder?"

"Maybe you're too caught up in our old ways. Maybe the difference is that you studied forestry, and I zoology."

"The infernal West infected you."

"Not everything you find there is bad."

"I can believe that. Their chocolate isn't bad, they make good cars, they publish more books than they can read.

They like to go to war with Muslim-ruled countries."

"Islam can't rule, it's a religion."

"Oh, my dear brother. What's happened to you? One more prayer?"

***

"How do you feel?" asks the older brother.

"Fine," answers the younger one, somewhat faintly and without expression.

"Have your doubts passed?"

"I think so."

"You think so, or they really did?"

"I have none at the moment."

"Then we can't wait for them to return."

"Maybe not."

"Even though I decided we would activate the bomb close to Singapore, about two hundred kilometers east of the river on Sumatra where our victim is to start felling trees."

"We can wait a little more."

"It's no longer far away."

"We'll live a few more minutes."

"Is life on this side so important to you? Aren't you more excited about what awaits us on the other side?"

"It's not a matter of what excites me. I'm less than dust in the universe. I'm more worried about whether I'm acting so as to please Allah."

"You'll be one of the blessed. Don't forget that Allah punishes doubters most harshly."

"Tell me when to type in the code."

"You have the cell phone in your pocket, turned on and ready?"

"Yes."

"Don't forget that first I have to enter my part of the code. Then you have to enter yours, immediately. You didn't forget the number?"

"No, I didn't."

"I'll think of the deep respect of the group we formed. Every one embraced us in turn."

"I'll think of our father and the tiger talking on the edge of the primeval forest. At the last instant, I'll try to embrace both of them. And mom, too."

"I've said good-bye to all three."

"How many minutes do we have left?"

"Eight? Maybe less. When the icon on the map is alongside the crime scene."

"In the meantime, can I tell you a short story? It might mean something to you."

"Go ahead, dear brother."

"It's not actually a story. It happened."

"I'm listening."

"In a certain village—I don't know exactly where—a shepherd was on his way home when he ran into an emaciated, helpless puppy. He took pity on it, took it home, and started caring for it. As the puppy grew up, they became ever better friends, and when it was full grown, it started watching the flock. The shepherd was grateful, but the villagers kept warning him: Don't be stupid, it's not a dog but a wolf. One day it will attack you and kill you.' The shepherd didn't believe them. The dog really did look like a wolf, but it was friendly and had become his best companion. He alertly guarded the flock against the wolves in the area. Then one night, the shepherd was awakened by a terrible noise. He ran out and saw his dog by the door as he had never seen him before. Fresh blood was dripping from his mouth, and his teeth clenched a piece of fresh meat. The shepherd hurried around the corner and came upon five mauled sheep. He returned to the house, grabbed his gun, went back to the door, and shot the dog in the head. When he had calmed down somewhat, he went to see how many sheep the dog had killed. This time he took a light along and went a little further. At the fence, he came upon many dead sheep.

But among them he found five mauled wild wolves. His heart broke. He grasped that he had wrongfully killed his best friend."

The older brother is quiet for a time.

"An instructive story," he says.

"For us as well?"

"I don't see how."

"Too bad."

"The time has come, brother. We have to activate the bomb."

"Right."

"It's time. We'll see each other in heaven."

"Do you have the phone in your hand?"

The young brother pulls out his phone and turns it on. "Yes."

"God bless us. As soon as I enter my three numbers, you have to enter yours."

"Farewell, world."

The older brother enters 373. The younger brother enters 383.

They wait. Nothing happens. The plane continues on its course for Singapore.

"Something went wrong," says the younger brother.

"You entered the wrong number. Did you forget it?"

"The group leader gave one to each of us. He didn't tell you mine or me yours. We were supposed to keep the numbers to ourselves."

"What did you enter?"

"And you?"

"The number I was assigned. 373. You?"

"I was assigned the same number."

"Did you enter it? Try again."

The younger brother once more enters 383. The plane continues on its course to Singapore.

"Something went wrong," says the younger brother.

"You entered the wrong number." He grabs the

younger brother's phone out of his hands and checks the calls. "You entered 383! Twice! Why?"

"I was clumsy."

"You entered the wrong number on purpose. You won't get away with it. I'm going to put the correct number in now."

He enters 373. Nothing happens. The plane continues on its course. "What now?"

"It probably only works if you enter the second number immediately after the first. If you make a mistake, the detonating system turns off."

The older brother takes a deep breath and is quiet for a while. Tears slowly start to run down his cheeks.

"Sorry," says the younger brother.

"Why did you do that?"

"I'll tell you," says the younger brother. "And then you can kill me, as you were ordered. I know you were ordered to. A while ago I overheard the conversation between a father and his eight-year old son sitting two rows ahead. You know, the one who screamed hysterically for several minutes before the doctor injected him with a sedative."

"And?"

"I asked myself whether I have the right to prevent the child from seeing his mom when he so misses her. Who gives me the right? Do I give it to myself? Because so far I haven't received authority in a message over a divine signature saying, 'Kill these people.'"

"Oh, dear brother, you really don't understand that this is war? Do you know how many civilians, including children, have died in battle? And how many more will?"

"I don't want to be one of those who kill innocent children. There are twenty-seven on this plane. I counted them."

"Not even at the cost of your own life?"

"Not even at the cost of my own life."

"I received instructions to kill you if you sabotage the plan at the last minute."

"I know. You have a syringe with poison in your pocket, and you can shove it into my thigh at any moment."

The older brother is silent.

"I won't, dear brother. Even though I was ordered to. I seem to be starting to understand your story about the shepherd and the wolf."

"If you don't kill me, the group will kill both of us."

"Better that than for me to kill you. Remember how as children we secretly watched our father talking with the tiger?"

"I can see it vividly."

"And after the forest burned and our parents and tiger friend died we asked ourselves who are the greater beasts, people or animals?"

"Did we find an answer?"

"I think we did. At least for today, people have become more human."

"At the cost of our lives."

"Wouldn't we have died if we detonated the bomb?"

***

"Dear passengers," the captain's voice comes over the intercom. "Please fasten your seatbelts. We're in an area of stronger than usual turbulence. Crew members, take your seats and fasten your seatbelts."

"Dear passengers," the head steward comes on. "You heard the captain's announcement. Please follow it strictly. We hope to get through the area of dangerous turbulence as soon as possible and land in Singapore in half an hour, as scheduled. There is no reason to panic, even if we are strongly, even severely affected. We are flying into the heart of a storm that we weren't able to avoid. I would like to assure you that a lightning strike, which you'll recognize by a loud metallic bang on the body of the plane, cannot cause hazardous damage. Crosswinds are a greater danger. A sudden airflow can thrust the plane upwards, as if flying vertically. Or plunge it into a vacuum below, as if it had lost its buoyancy. Neither event is catastrophic, though it will be quite unpleasant. Therefore I repeat: remain seated with your seatbelts fastened as long as the sign is illuminated. Thank you for your understanding."

www.ingramcontent.com/pod-product-compliance
Lightning Source LLC
Chambersburg PA
CBHW020353170426
43200CB00005B/145